GUTTER TO GLORY

by

Kerri Douglas

It was the end of January 2020, when I received a

phone call from Petra Salva OBE, who is the director of

rough sleeping at the homeless charity, St Mungo's.

I had been feeling really deflated, because I hadn't

been asked to share my story since it had been

published in the Times Christmas Appeal 2018, for

Mungo's.

I'm a firm believer that there is power in the

testimony and sharing mine can bring a lot of hope to a

lot of people. So, I was excited to take the call, however,

nothing could prepare me for what was about to come...

Needing to escape the sound of the children fighting in the background, I slipped out the backdoor and locked it behind me so I could speak with Petra properly. After the pleasantries Petra got straight to the point! "I know it is short notice, but are you free to come and speak in Parliament next week and again in March?"

It felt like someone had let off a firework inside of me as I exploded with excitement. Before the reality hit me! I am a single parent on benefits! And have no way of paying the fare down to London from the Wirral and back again. Then there is the fact I would need at least

48 hours of childcare to consider for my nine-year-old twins.

I had to politely decline the invitation, something that could be potentially life changing was literally at my disposal, I was gutted by the time we had ended the call.

Still excited from the fact that I had been asked though, as soon as I ended the call with Petra, I called Sandy. Now, Sandy is my children's paternal grandmother and although there is no contact with my children's father, Sandy is like a mum to me and is a huge support when it comes to the children.

I could not wait to tell her about my near

parliament experience...

I can't quite remember the full details, so to cut it

short, by the end of the conversation, my hopes were

built once more as I scrolled through my contacts list, to

find Petra's number.

Sandy had told me she would have the children,

and I could go to London to speak in the Houses of

Parliament! As I waited for Petra to answer I was

praying that it was not too late, and that they had not

found someone else to do it.

To my relief, Petra answered and informed me that it was all good and she was looking forward to seeing me next week in Parliament...

Oh my gosh, how could this be? I kept pinching myself to make sure it was real. If you had have told me twelve years ago that I would be speaking in parliament about the life I was living back then, I would have laughed in your face.

Twelve years ago, I was sleeping on the streets of Westminster, taking hundreds of pounds worth of drugs a day, wasting away in a life of chaos. Sleeping in cardboard boxes and begging passersby for change! Fast forward to 2020 and life is the complete opposite.

How could this be though? How can one go from the lowest of the low, to a complete reversal in ways of living? Do you want to know how I went from sleeping on the pavements in Westminster, to speaking in the Houses of Parliament?

Keep reading...

Chapter One – Just A Girl

It was the 2nd of May 1984... Obviously I can't remember the day I was born, so I need to give a bit of hearsay for the first part of this chapter. My mum and father were together when I was born, although unmarried.

They were in an intimate relationship. All I really know about this day is that my name came from a song, that played on my mum's mind. "Hey, Kerri Anne, what's your game now can anybody play?"

It is ironic really because all my life I have played a game of chicken across the tracks. Jumping from gap to gap in life, like a little dare devil so lucky not to fall down the hole. Although I have fallen down that hole many of times. I have always found a way to climb out!

Back to the story though...

Okay, so I was the youngest child of my mothers, she had two other daughters before me. Sadly, my oldest sister died at the incredibly young age of six months. I never got to meet my sister, but there has always been a place in my heart for her.

My other older sister I do not really want to talk about through this book, more for respect for her privacy. I also want to honor my mother the same way. We all have our difficulties in life, who are we to judge another from their mistakes, instead we must learn from them.

My Father was in my life for around ten months, before he and my mother split violently. The split led to me not seeing my father again until later in my life. We will get to that in a bit!

My mother had met a man, shortly after the split with my father. A man she went on to marry. That man became my first stepdad. However, by the time I was eighteen months old. That relationship had also deteriorated due to violence. One thing I will say about my mum is she has the strength of ten men and will give back just as hard as she gets. One of the things I received from her genetics and I am proud of it!

My mum has her insecurities for her own reasons and who knows she may even write her own book one day! Due to those insecurities, she finds it difficult to be alone without a man in her life. Being a single parent was never going to be a label on my mum.

I was around two years old when my mum had started a relationship with another man. My mum went on to marry that man and he became my DAD! (You will see my reason of capitalizing as you read on) ...

I am going to skip on a couple of years because, my memories are vague, I remember we moved a couple of times, but my real memories began in Bensham Crescent. I can't say specifically how old I was when we moved to Bensham, the school my sister and I went to, was my first actual school so I guess I must have been around five.

My parents seemed happy together and we were one big happy family. Dad would talk about adopting us, then came the proposal which my mum accepted. It was perfect.

The Big Day - September 1st 1990...

My sister and I were bridesmaids at the wedding with my auntie. It was a beautiful day. The bridesmaid dress I wore was blue and my hair was in two French plaits. After the ceremony there was a reception for all ages at a local pub. Then later in the evening there was an adult only party.

In the evening when everyone was at the party, my sister and I were being babysat by our great grandmother. She was extremely deaf and quite elderly and frail.

Along with my great nan there was a cousin through marriage staying over too. A female cousin that was around ten years older than me. I was six at the time of my parents' wedding.

The house in Bensham was a three bedroomed property, my sister and I had our own bedrooms. My bedroom was right at the top of the stairs, neighboring the living room.

Whilst lying in bed that evening my thoughts racing ten to the dozen from the day. An excited little six-year-old so happy that we were a proper family.

Mid thought, my bedroom door opened, followed by my cousin peering her head around the corner of my door. "You Ok" She asked as she came in, I do not really know what we talked about, but I just remember that I was quite happy rabbling on to her about the events that had taken place that day. As she climbed into my bed, I felt fine, no reason to be alarmed, right?

This was my cousin it is fine to share a bed. The conversation soon changed as my cousin began to tell me about her pregnancy. She was going to have a baby! This brought me excitement. A natural feeling, I guess.

She went on to say that, when the baby came it would have to drink milk from her breasts. I had no idea what she was talking about I was six, my mother had not got to the birds and the bees talk yet.

My cousin asked me to perform oral sex on her. She told me that certain acts would be "Kissing her baby" or testing her breasts for milk. I feel sick just typing this part of my life. For so many years I have felt such shame, but I was only a six-year-old girl!!...

She went on to tell me that it was a secret that she was pregnant, and I could not tell anyone, I did as I was told. Even when it became apparent that she was not having a baby as time went by, I have always kept her secret. Until now!

I'm sorry to be so graphic it makes me want to hurl reading it too, but to be fair how do you tell that sort of story? This event did not affect me till years later in my life, and if I am honest it haunts me to this day, but who knows me sharing this with you, may bring me some healing and freedom, and not to mention in hope that it brings freedom for someone else.

After my mum and dad married, they both worked like dogs to provide for us. Mum had 3 jobs on the go at one point. Although they did their best to provide for us, they were unable to provide us with their time. Something I know they both regret now.

Due to the overbearing work schedule, my nan would look after us. Our day would look like this...

We would wake up, as mum and dad were leaving for work, my nan who lived a few doors away. Would come and get us in our nightdresses to take us to her house.

When we got there, we would get ready for school and have breakfast. Then off we went to school. At three thirty when the school day was over, back we went to nana's house where we would have dinner. Mum and Dad would then come and collect us. Home we went with little time to spare before bed.

My nan had many children including two sets of twins. I do not know exactly how many children my nan bore as she lost some of her offspring through childbirth including one of each set of twins. However, she had five healthy children consisting of three boys and two girls when I was growing up.

The youngest two of her children were teenagers at the time my nana used to look after us. So, they were more like elder siblings than auntie and uncle.

As siblings do, they used to torment me and call me stupid and goad me to tears. They would find amusement in setting the Yorkshire terrier dogs on me by yanking on my cardigan saying "gets, gets."

I remember being dragged down the stairs by the gruesome twosome as my family just laughed. They are the smallest dogs, but boy are they vicious!

I would cry out, which fueled their behavior. In their minds there is no harm, they were just messing, but if I did it to their children. Well, that would be completely different now. I do not hold a grudge, but I will say that I know their behavior was wrong.

They were young and did not really have a clue about the real impact that their constant tormenting was going to have on me.

Around a year after my parent's had married, we moved into an area that was alien to us, it was a house with two great big gardens. Maple Road, one of my favorite homes.

Maple road was a very spacious three-bedroom house. It was my dream home. My sister and I shared a room, and the spare room was our playroom. Everything was perfect, we were a real proper family in a real proper family home.

So, I thought! We were too young to see the cracks appearing in my parents' marriage. Around 1992 they split for the first time. Due to the separation, my mum decided she wanted to move back to her birthplace in East London. So, all packed up, off we went.

Shortly after we arrived in London, we stayed at an old boyfriend of hers flat, behind Bow road police station. He was a nice man, a lot older than my mum but he was nice. It soon became apparent that this was a new boyfriend of my mothers, and that this was now our new family.

I always felt like I was betraying my dad, by playing happy families with someone else but in all honesty, I did not really understand what was going on. By this time, I was used to different men being around.

We were only there for around six months; I remember celebrating my eighth birthday in that house. Although it was not long after that we moved into a bed and breakfast in Streatham because the relationship had broken down.

Well! Have you ever been in temporary accommodation, provided by the local authority because you were facing homelessness? That is basically what this bed and breakfast was.

We were homeless! My mum, my sister and me. It was just the three of us for the first time ever. The council had placed us into this temporary accommodation. It was disgusting!

My sister would call it bug city! It was one room, basically your average studio room with a little en-suite bathroom attached. Not that anyone would even dare to go in there. In fear of being bombarded by cockroaches. It really was traumatic, the thought of the bugs crawling all over us while we slept.

The place was overrun by cockroaches. I am still petrified of the things now.

We only stayed there one night. Then off we went to my grandads' house. My mum's biological father. He was like the BFG so tall and kind. We only stayed there a little while before we moved into a squat around the corner from him.

Over the course of a couple of months my mum became very chaotic in her search to meet the next person we would be calling dad. So chaotic she would go out on the town and leave us alone with a neighbor looking in on us from time to time.

That is how the music man came along. I am trying so hard to not mention anyone's names here but even I am beginning to lose track now. The music man was called Simon, he was a partner we only met once so it really does not matter if I name him. I call him the music man because when we went to his house, there were musical instruments everywhere. We were around 8 and 9 at the time.

The guy was also on top of the pops once too. This was the first relationship to split our family apart. With my mum spending more and more time at Simons we became extremely neglected.

One day my sister had enough of my mum just leaving us overnight to go and see her boyfriend. So, she called my nana, to come and get us.

I remember her sobbing because she had enough. Bearing in mind she was not even a ten-year-old.

What felt like the next day, my nana and uncle were in front of us in our living room getting ready to take us back to Newcastle.

My mum did not seem too bothered and just let us go. This was the first time my nana applied for custody of my sister and me.

It was around 1993 I was only around eight or nine, we had been living with my nana for a couple of months.

She had applied for a residence order so that she could have complete guardianship for me and my sister.

My mum failing to appear in court automatically gave my nana the rights. It was about six months later that my mum finally came to get us. To which time it was too late.

I remember the day like it was yesterday. I had just got in from school and my nana was waiting. "I've got some good news" she said. I was excited to hear what she had to tell me. "Your mums coming" she went on to say. I just broke into tears, a flood of emotion just washed over me.

"Why are you crying?" my nana asked, "I don't know" I replied, I am just happy! In that moment, my nana gave me a hug, she rarely expressed emotion, so I clenched on tighter to keep me topped up until the next time she felt the need to give me a cuddle.

I asked if I could stay up late till my mum arrived, but my nana declined. She told me that my mum would not be arriving until it was extremely late. So, no! It was completely out of the question. Although I was not allowed to stay up, there was no way that I was getting any sleep that night! I of course was still awake when my mum arrived around midnight.

All those feelings that I expected to feel were nowhere in sight. I felt numb!

My mother was here, sitting right there in front of me. After all this time she was there. Should I hug her I thought to myself, in that thought process, I found myself making way to my mum.

I sat on her knee, it felt weird because I was a big girl now. Almost nine, however an incredibly young nine. It was a very brief moment of reconciliation, before she told me to get off, but it was enough to make me feel something again.

I got sent to bed and was out like a light, feeling content because my mum was home. My mother was staying at her little sister's house at the bottom of the street, we were living in at first.

My mum was trying her best to convince my nana she was up to parenting my sister and me. She had got a house in Scotswood which is a little distance from my nanas house in Blaydon. However, mum was determined she wanted us back.

My nana would let us visit at first, then eventually allowed us to go back and live with her. Before we officially went back to live there, I remember coming home from school and my nana told me she had some news for me. This again? What could it be?

My nana said that my mum was going to take me to meet my dad, I looked at her saying okay, but he only lives down the street. No, she said! Your real dad.

So, basically, she was talking about the man who played a part in my conception. The man who had not seen me since I was a babe in arms. So, it turns out, my biological father lived about three streets away from our new house in Scotswood.

When we first arrived at his house, I recall being shy. Then he pulled out a Sega master system and I was putty in his hands. By the end of the visit, he was the best thing since sliced bread. I had two dads now how lucky was I.

As these days played out, I had no idea the impact that it was having on my dad. Not my father but my dad.

The man who had raised me as his own since I was two years old. He is my real dad, my absolute hero! The only man that you will ever hear me call DAD! It is only now that I realize how much it hurt him when I had a brief relationship with my biological father.

I must highlight on the word BRIEF, that is exactly what it was! It was the year Jurassic Park was on in the cinema, I remember because it was the last place we went for our contact. So, from just before my ninth birthday in May 1993 up until July 1993.

After a quick two-month fix of biological love and then off goes my father. I was very used to change in my life already so; it did not really faze me that this man I barely knew was gone.

I do remember asking when I was going to see him again though occasionally as time went by. We lived in three houses in Scotswood, two that were more or less next door to each other. The third house was about five streets away. That house... I recall as the house of horrors.

Chapter Two – Who Cares

We moved to the third house I think in the late summer of 1993. It was around the same time the contact ended with my biological father. My mum had done a 360-degree spin and was now more chaotic than her last breakdown in London.

Like before, mum would go out once a week on the town, Thursdays to be exact, leaving us to fend for ourselves, with a neighbor looking in. We were older now; I was nine and my sister would be eleven at the end of the summer.

Not quite old enough to be left alone till the early hours of the morning, but like I said my mum has always had her own demons to face.

I also want to add that my mum was diagnosed with bipolar disorder when I was around seventeen! So, I ask you to please consider this fact as you continue to read on.

Back to the story though!

Okay, picture the scene... A nine-year-old with no boundaries, left home alone with no parental guidance. If you picture the kid from problem child and put him in the movie home alone, you may see where I'm going with this.

So, every Thursday mum would get ready to go out on the town. She would have a bath; blow dry her hair then fix up her makeup and off she went as regular as clockwork.

When she went out, she would ask the neighbor in the downstairs flat to look in on us. At first it was all safe and sound, we would play out till it got dark then come in and later go to sleep in mums bed awaiting her return. Over a space of about two months this occurred.

Now, where we lived was one of the roughest parts of Newcastle. So, it's safe to say I was easily influenced by poor peer choices. Let's face it, all I had witnessed in my life up until now, Bad Ass was becoming first nature.

I used to get up to all sorts from smoking the joints my mum left in the ashtray, to joining the bigger kids in the street as they got up to mischief. After about three weeks, one night my mum came home drunk, stripped, and got straight into bed.

Then in the early hours of the morning she was awoken by a man in the bedroom crouched at her bed, trying to cut the rings off her fingers, she had at least one on each finger. When she woke up, she automatically jumped up and chased the man out of the house and halfway down the street, completely oblivious to the fact she was naked.

Now, I would personally like to think that would have been the awakening needed for her behavior to change. Unfortunately, that was not the case.

Due to this incident, my dad had let us look after his rottweiler Bruno. He was as soft as muck but hopefully, due to his breeds reputation his bark would be enough of a scare tactic to keep burglars at bay.

The following week mum had decided to go out again, and left us on our own with the neighbor looking in. It was all good because, we had Bruno now too, it was all going to be completely safe and above board. As usual mum came into us sleeping in her bed, where she would join us.

I'm not quite sure what happened this night but somehow, someone managed to break in. Only this time they stole my dad's baby! Yup, they took the dog.

Bruno was a first-year wedding anniversary present from my mum. My dad adored him! He was a full pedigree rottweiler, and the perfect example of man's best friend. As you can imagine my dad was absolutely devastated.

After a short time, it could have been days or maybe even over a week later, the lady who lived downstairs that would watch in on us, informed my mum she knew where Bruno was. I don't know the whole in's and out, but I remember the woman's cousin Lee was an absolute hero because he somehow managed to retrieve our Bruno.

To prevent anything like this happening again my dad took Bruno home that night, so we were back to just being three vulnerable females under one roof. Around two weeks later after a brief retreat, mum had decided she was going out. It was Thursday and it had been a couple of weeks.

This time was different though! This time she asked the lady downstairs to babysit us properly. It's strange because I remember so clearly of this night.

We went to the lady's relatives house for some reason. To which Lee came into the house, the man who got our dog back. Apparently, he lived there. I remember him making a big spectacle about getting in the bath, like he wanted us to know that's where he was.

It seemed like a very long time that he was in there, but when he returned, he looked exactly as he did when he left. His hair was dry and clothes the same. Even at nine years old I was extremely observant, I have no idea why, but It does come in useful though.

Not long after Lee returned from the bathroom, it was time for us to go home. It was Lee and his girlfriend that took us back. Upon walking up the stairs we knew something wasn't quite right. Then, we reached the living room to find that we had been completely burgled.

With no mobile phones in those days, just the good old-fashioned land line there was no way of contacting my mum, so we just had to wait till she came home.

To be honest most of the night from that point on is a bit of a blur, maybe because that was a memory, I have desperately tried so hard to forget. Not long after that night though we finally moved! Back to Blaydon into the same street as my Nana.

Rebelling from traumatic events, my mother and I began to clash big time! I resented her so much. I had zero respect towards her, and she had no authority over me. I just wanted the woman to love me, but she didn't know how. But she knew how to love my sister which irritated me even more.

Christmas came and went, then a New Year arrived and in early 1994, my auntie and her sister-in-law decided to take a trip to London to visit my cousin Shell. On that visit, my auntie met a man and started a long-distance relationship. Then, the man and his friend came to visit my auntie at her home in Newcastle.

After a short time, my auntie moved to Erith in Kent to live with the man. Not long after my mum took us for a three-week holiday during summer break. In which time she started a relationship with my aunties, boyfriends, friend, who came to Newcastle that time. I know it all sounds confusing! Right? Wait till you read on later it gets a whole lot more confusing!

During our three-week holiday, mum had decided that she too wanted to move to Kent, and that thought very quickly materialized into a move into her new boyfriend's house.

Wow did this anger me! I hated the fact my mum had once again just picked us up and carried us three hundred miles and taken us away from my dad. All for another man! How dare she!

I started a primary school at the end of our street in the September 1994, I hated that too! I was bullied for the whole year I was there because I was different. Having a very strong Geordie accent, nobody could understand me, which led to even more ridicule.

My last year of primary school was probably one of the toughest years of my childhood. My mother and I were so volatile towards each other and I felt so much rage because I have never been able to handle my emotions well.

Not to mention the fact that my neglected appearance and my sellotape, thick, national health spectacles, that were fixed to my head with an elastic band, because I constantly lost them accidently on purpose! Was opening me up for being bullied.

Trying so desperate to fit in, I would do things that were wrong, like smoke, steal and cause trouble. All to make me look good in front of the cool kids, trying my best to claim acceptance.

Along with the mischief came constant battles with my mum and then one day she just flipped. It was sometime in 1995, I was approaching eleven years old, somehow volatile yet innocent. I was angered by mum so easily. One day she had caught me with one of her lighters and just lost control.

Then she walked into the kitchen, after giving me a hiding, she almost slit her wrists in anger, then called social services and told them to come and get me. My mum was desperate, saying if you don't come and get her, I'll either hurt her or myself.

After a short period of time, we had to attend a meeting at the Howbury Centre. As we waited in the lobby, there was a lady with a little mixed raced boy, he was around two with a head full of curly hair.

I have always loved babies and toddlers, a natural instinct within me would arise to interact with the little people. I played with the little boy as we waited, my mum looked so lovingly at the little boy too. It is weird because I know my mum loves me in her weird way, but she never looked at me the same way.

Something else I have always resented is the fact my mum always shows love to other people's kids but never the same for me. Like I said though, I know she loves me in her own way, so I'm kind of over that now.

Back to the story! As we waited, and I played with the little boy. I remember thinking how it would be nice to live with this lady and her little boy. When the social worker came in, she said shall we go through, to my joy! Jayne and Danny came in too.

I was over the moon! I felt bad on my mum, but it was as if she didn't want me, so it was okay. At least I was going to live with someone that was nice, and that I already liked!

Jaynes house was different, it was filled with peace and love, not like the hippy kind, but the kind of warm peaceful family love. It felt so natural.

It very quickly became apparent that Jayne and Glen her husband were Christian's. Every Sunday they would attend a little Pentecostal Church in Woolwich, South East London. I absolutely loved it.

Everyone would dance up and down the aisles, singing Hallelujah, Praise the Lord. It was on fire! I had never seen such joy in all of my life.

Each week we went, and I loved it more and more. So, I asked my mum if I could be baptized, she declined stating if God was real, why did Rebecca die? At that age I had no answer to such a question, so I never asked again.

I lived there well over a year; I was actually sad to leave when I returned to my mum's care.

However, I was only home with my mum a matter of weeks before I was back in care at Jaynes house. Only this time was different, she had two other girls with special needs, that required her undivided attention.

I became very insecure and felt as though I was unwanted, the second time round. That was the beginning of my runaway days. I left Jaynes care and that was the start of many placements to come. Placement's where there was no love, just selfish motive. The more I moved around, the more unstable I became.

Running away at every opportunity I became what is known as a prolific absconder. I hated being in care, I hated the fact that I was so easily discarded yet, my older sibling was held so close like a porcelain doll.

One day whilst living in this foster placement, I got into a big argument with the foster carer.
which resulted in me being arrested. Fourteen and detained in custody for losing my rag, with a wannabe goody too shoes. Another label was added to the growing blacklist, now I was also.
known as a criminal.

I was charged with criminal damage and received six months conditional discharge as my
sentence from the court. I only kicked a vase which was already broken. To be fair at this point I had grown into my label of problem child well.

In reflection though, looking back yes, I may have had chronic behavioral issues but instead of understanding and addressing why, I was palmed off to whoever would have me next. Due to my prolific running away and the list of registered foster carers and children's homes coming to an end, I had to be moved out of area a couple of times.

This is something that did not go down well with me. The fact I was miles away in the
countryside or by the coast meant running away would require more effort. It did not stop me trying though. My family had completely washed their hands with me because of my behavior and it felt like social services had just palmed me off out of area for an easier life.

I wanted to be at home with my real mum, instead of with the pretend wannabes the social worker kept placing me with. To be honest when I look back, I think what a little minx I was, always thought I knew what was best. Bold and stubborn were a trait that I had not yet mastered.

Chapter Three – Runaway

Running away became part of my daily routine, as well as bunking off school to go up west on the train. We lived in a place called Erith in Kent, which was about 40 minutes away on the train. So, every day instead of going to school I would bunk off, then bunk the train and runaway to the West End. I was thirteen and full of angst towards peers and would do anything to get a reaction.

One day, I'd run away from a foster placement to go up west. I loved going to the west end in hunt for famous people. My favorite haunt was sound republic, opposite Leicester Square.

Back in the nineties they used to host MTV select there, you were guaranteed to see someone famous. I actually believed that I would one day become famous if I hung out there long enough. I often stayed up west till the last train, but something was different this day. I went up the west end and missed the train home.

That was when I met my street family. Even to this day, there is a community of homeless people that congregate and sleep under Charing cross station. When I was thirteen, there was around twenty people that slept there!

It was mid to late nineties and carboard city had been eliminated to make way for the upcoming money-making attractions in waterloo. So, all the homeless people that lived in cardboard city moved to Charing cross station, the back of the savoy hotel and underneath Waterloo bridge.

Although the community became scattered, it was a family that stuck together. A family that I instantly felt drawn to.

Maggie Thatcher's lost boys mainly. Runaway kids from care, there were only a few women though. I would say there was about seven females in total in all the communities combined.
There was an elder woman that everyone called mum, she really was like a mum to us all.
The men were like brothers, looking out for us ladies.

There was only a couple, that I felt comfortable around, when it came to the men. The ones that I did feel comfortable with, protected me from so many dangers as I continued to runaway to the streets. I do not know what it was, that kept drawing me into that life, it just felt fitting.

I had made lots of friends on the street mainly through the soup vans that used to attend the Strand every night. We were like a family all looking out for each other.
I did get a slap once for being too young. And I was told to go home because I didn't belong there. The truth is, that was the only place in my mind, I did belong.

As the years went by, I became quite popular with the police. They would come and remove me from my begging spot outside the NatWest bank on the strand, to take me home to my current foster carers.

I used to find it quite amusing, they would drop me off home and by the time they got back to their patrol on the Strand, I would be sitting in the very same spot, begging for my McDonalds. Yes, I know! Good way to spend taxes, right?!... I'm only joking!

I'm not denying I was an absolute little bitch. I even got Bitch No.1 tattooed on my arm at aged fifteen, thinking it was clever. Oooh, if I knew then what I know now!!

I feel like this is a good point to highlight the fact that I was a kid with no morals or awareness of boundaries, nor did I have any ability to consider the ethics behind my behavior. Also, we have now uncovered that I have ADHD which explains a lot of my behaviors.

I had no love shown to me as a child, I was just a big inconvenience to all. Cast aside like an old boot, as my grandad used to say. I continued to run away on a regular basis, to which point social services had run out of placements to house me in.

Which was when I moved to Eastbourne in East Sussex, the one place that I somehow managed to settle in. Miles away from the west end, and miles away from my family, a clean break from everything.

The thing is, I was not impressed with this move! There was no way I was moving all this way. My poor social worker Eileen had to listen to me cursing all the way from Slade Green in Kent to this new foster placement on the seafront of Eastbourne, which was approximately an hour's drive away.

I remember the drive down to Eastbourne like it was yesterday. I was adamant I was not staying there. My poor social worker was at her wits end. I gave her the run around for sure.

When we pulled up outside this huge four-story house on the seafront, I dug my heels into my seat and refused to get out of the car. At this time in my life, I was fourteen and full of bad attitude.

I had become the master at wrapping social workers around my little finger. For sure this was going to work, Eileen would get fed up with waiting and eventually, she will take me home, she can't physically move me! I remember thinking to myself.

I so had this! The next thing I knew there was a lady outside the car, she knocked on the window and asked if I wanted a fag? I just remember being so taken back by this lady who didn't know me from Adam, yet she knew exactly how to calm me right there and then.

The truth is behind the bad attitude I was just a girl, craving for someone to get me. Someone to understand me. Heck let's be honest I just needed to feel like someone loved me and not the hefty paycheck.

The lady gave me a cigarette and reassured me that everything was going to be ok. We both stood up from the curb, I took a deep breath and went into my new home with my new foster mum Bev...

In Bev's Words...

"So, there I was in my lounge with a couple of social workers. "I'm sorry, said Kerry's social worker. She's refusing to come in. I looked out the window, my heart tweaked. That poor girl, it's not surprising, sat in the car across the road I could see the figure of a teenaged girl in the car head down.

We waited. She never came in. I grabbed a packet of cigarettes left the house crossed the road, knocked on

the car window. 'Would you like a cigarette, I'm Bev"
You looked at me, I felt you were weighing me up for a
second. You got out the car and we sat on the edge of
the pavement and short conversation that I can't quite
remember.

You decided to come in. Moving on several months, and
after a few hiccups I won't mention unless you want me
to privately. You definitely changed it was a slow change
but a change, nevertheless. You appeared a little more
in control. Little easier to reason with. Less angry with
yourself. We will always have a soft spot for Kerri" –
Beverly Arkle

I shocked many people whilst living at this placement. I
always felt like I was a part of the family unit. It was all
good for around eighteen months then things turned
sour. I became extremely close to Bev, so close she was
like a proper mum to me.

The only thing was, I wasn't her only foster child. When
new kids came, I felt threatened and intimidated not to
mention the fact I was a hormonal teenager. I never got
on with other kids in care, the worst was when I lived in

the kid's homes, I was always fighting and getting kicked out for going too far.

My natural response was hurt before you get hurt. So, when new kids came to Bev's that same instinct would surface. Only I didn't hurt the kids, I hurt the care giver instead. I still have regrets of my behavior towards the end of my placement at Bev's house.

I was about to turn sixteen when I officially left Bev's care, I remember us both being devastated by my destruction. Destruction became my middle name from then on...

Eileen had found me a placement in Abbey Wood, they were brand new foster carers and couldn't wait to have me. If only they knew then what they knew now...

I was a nightmare for them. Chris was the nicest lady, with such a heart of gold. Ray was a bit firmer, he scared me a little in a dad kind of way. Nevertheless, they were so kind and caring, and me being me I took advantage.

A few days before my 16th birthday I decided to run away and join the fun fair. I had met a guy and fallen in love, besotted was an understatement. I was prepared to give up everything and travel the fair with him. The thing was, he wasn't that into me.

We travelled from west end to Hereford which is where he literally binned me off. Although I'm the sort of person to wear my heart on my sleeve, my tolerance to emotional pain is phenomenal. I guess it's all those years of feeling unloved by the people who should love you.

So, there I was in Hereford feeling pretty sorry for myself, whilst poor Chris was at home worried sick about me. Having been missing for days on end. I had to go home, with a huge slice of humble pie. I remember I had been wearing a white outfit for days, it stunk and was filthy with dirt.

I remember the looks of horror on the train from Manchester Piccadilly all the way to Charing Cross as I sat in squalor with my head down in shame. Upon arrival at London Charing Cross I made way to Charing cross police station.

I knew that if I represented myself as a runaway, they would call the emergency social worker, who would then call my carers. I remember the moment when Chris saw me again, she was just so relieved to see me safe and well. I'd never seen that look of relief in someone's eye before, this woman actually cared about me!

Unfortunately, I was beyond control at this point, and my time a Chris and Ray's house was short lived. Chris in particular has always had a place in my heart though, even to this day she is a part of my life, encouraging me into greatness.

Here is a statement from Chris...

*****

We had been approved as foster carers and with having had no placements from the November, we asked if we could foster someone short term so we would know if it was the right thing for us before making a big commitment to long term care for someone.

Along came Kerri on a short-term basis so excited to finally be doing what we had wanted to do. Everything was fine at the beginning. Kerri stayed in a few nights then the running started to the fair is where she went and stayed. Police were regularly looking for her I presume bringing her home, but I can't remember.

I remember a phone call from a night duty social worker who said they had found you, but she wasn't prepared to go get you and bring you back as she remembered you very well and how you would kick off in her car. Think you had to stay overnight at the police station not sure but presume so.

I always worried where were you, were you ok, a mixture of emotions when you have someone you are looking after. I remember one morning I had a phone call very early from the police in London at Charing Cross to say they had you there and would I go and get you.

Gemma had the day off college to go with me as I don't know my way around London. We got you and brought you back here on the train and I was mortified with what you were wearing, a white trouser suit all in one that had a bit that hung from the back down dragging on the floor and was filthy dirty.

Another memory every time you came back the police would have to come round and do a debrief and I always remember what you said to one policeman talk to the hand the face doesn't want to know, I was mortified as it sounded so rude to me and he was just doing his job. It was the first time I had heard that saying but always stayed with me.

You said you wanted to stop running and wanted to stay long term with us. You promised you wouldn't run again. I spoke to my link worker who agreed it was ok. You were very pleased, and that afternoon put your stamp on your room. Put up posters put clothes in your wardrobe. We explained as you had continually run that this was your last chance, we felt we were not doing what we came into foster care for, so we hope that this was it.

That evening off you went and so the placement ended. I can't remember how or where you went after us. I can't remember your social worker either going back eighteen years!

* * * * * *

My childhood and upbringing were key in what you are about to read in the next few chapters. Behavior is learnt and unfortunately the only behavior I ever learnt growing up, was how to be unstable.

With no idea on how to stay in one place for a long period, my idea of settlement was being on my toes. Despite being under a full care plan until I was twenty-one, I was released from care at age seventeen with no place to go. I showed no signs of stability, therefore the local authority had no more they could offer me.

When you get discharged from care, you move into supported accommodation. It is either a shared house with other care leavers or someone who owns a house, lets you live there under agreement with the leaving care team.

I had a different social worker; her name was Janis and boy did she put up with some crap from me. She housed me in a few supported lodgings, but somehow, I would mess it up. I had no rules, no boundaries, and no curfew but I did have a key and an uncontrollable urge to do whatever I wanted.

I had complete freedom; nobody was ever going to tell me what to do ever again! The only thing is, it is not as good as it sounds. I would go up west for nights on end, begging to make some money, to buy my shopping. Or I would join the fair when it was in season.

Then leave the fair at the end of the season. To end up on the doorstep of the leaving care team at the Howbury center in Slade Green, Kent.

I would sit in the lobby for hours on end, demanding to see Janis my social worker or Jacquie the manager. I needed a placement, and I was not going anywhere until I got it.

Fortunately for me I was under a full care plan, and the local authority were my legal guardians and had no choice but to accommodate me with the necessary support until I was twenty-one. Which by the way they neglected to maintain in a different area of the country!

Although I was no longer in care, the local authority had an obligation to keep me safe.

Then one day, I had ran out of places to go, there was literally nothing more they could offer me. All of my unstable behavior had finally caught up with me! Aged seventeen with my whole life ahead of me...

All I felt was abandoned. With no resources left in Kent, I found myself up west again. Living in a real-life edition of Oliver Twist.

*****

So, here I was seventeen, full of hurt, resentment and anger against the world for not loving me. I became more settled in, sleeping under Charing Cross train station. With a street family who got me. This is where I belonged. This was my destiny; I was living the real life of the artful dodger.

With mega insecurities and settlement issues, I was always on my toes. The ability to settle was just not in me. My whole life I had moved around from house to house, school to school and have had various male figures trying to be my dad! And that was before I went into care.

Then, whilst in care I always felt like I was just a pay cheque to whoever would take me. So, when I was seventeen, I embraced rough sleeping fully and the added complexities that came with it. My bed was either under Charing cross station or under Westminster bridge in a cardboard house.

It was not long before I was sucked into the life of substance abuse, having ADHD one of the symptoms is impulse and the expectancy of substance abuse is high. So, when I was offered a pipe of crack one day I was hooked from the start.

It was a very short-lived addiction at that point, one that only lasted about six weeks.

When I was sleeping under the train station, I began a relationship with a guy called trigger. I had experienced crack for the first time, and we became partners in selling the Big Issue to raise money for the drug.

We were never intimate; we were more like best friends. I was what you call frigid and never wanted to go all the way. In fact, I was so frigid I never even snogged him. After a couple of weeks of waking up having a pipe, running around on the hamster wheel that came with the addiction. Beg, score, be high for twenty minutes and then go and do it all again. It quickly became unbearable.

I was on a comedown after days of abusing crack, needing to freshen up, I went to the connections at St, Martins to shower and have a cooked meal. This was back when The Connection at St' Martins was only for people aged 16-25. It was a drop-in for young people that were exposed to homelessness.

I was hyper this day, but like a delirious kind of hyper, I kept speaking in a weird American accent pretending I was not me. The staff, were alarmed by my behavior and the nasty cough that I had too, so they suggested I go to A&E.

I got admitted to St Thomas's Hospital in London and required ventilation. My chest had packed up from a serious infection, which was made worse, from my chronic crack use and sleeping out in the cold. As soon as I was fit enough though, the next day I was discharged back to the streets. The hospital could not wait to get the bed back and sterilized for its next occupant.

I just want to pause for thought a minute...

Okay, a seventeen-year-old, asthmatic, with a serious chest infection and evident mental health issues. Who also may I add is under a full care plan until she was twenty-one? Is in the hospital in need of ventilation, and care, yet she is discharged back to the streets with no follow up care plan in place, Is that even humane?!

Nobody actually gave a toss, what was the point of even being alive. Well, that was my thoughts anyway. I felt abandoned and neglected, something had to give. So, hating myself and the life I was living, it was time for me to call on my family. Well, my older sister to be precise.

I called my sister the next day and asked if I could go and stay with her for a couple of days, which to my surprise she agreed to. However, soon the novelty wore off and she became tired of me just being around doing nothing.

I knew I had to begin engaging with the social services in Gateshead, my place of birth. So, I approached them and made a connection to the area and my case was transferred from Kent to Newcastle. They told me I had to represent as homeless and sent me to the civic center to the homeless department. I was then placed in a temporary hostel in Belle Vue bank, and It was not long, before I had bagged myself a tidy little two bedroom flat, in the street behind my sister's house.

It was going to be amazing! It was going to be different! I was going to get my act together and grow up!...

Hmmm, guess how long that lasted!!

Not long at all! I was completely left to my own devices, which inevitably ended in chaos. I was so buzzing when I moved in. I lived in a fairytale world, thinking I could manage this tenancy like a big girl...

Being a care leaver, I was entitled to a leaving care grant of £1000 to set me up in my first flat. The social worker clearly had no faith in me though, she only let me have £300 of it. That was enough to start though.

I had a cooker, fridge freezer and a bed to sleep in. I also had a tv and sofa, so I was ok, the basics were there. Materialistically anyway! Because when it came to common sense that basic was missing.

Time for another pause for thought!

If you look back to what you have read so far, would you give a girl like me in that mentality, a full tenancy and leave her to her own devices? I am hoping you agree with me when I say "NO!!!"

I painted the floorboards with white gloss paint, which might have looked ok, if I had painted from the corner to the door! Instead, I painted in reverse and ended up stuck in the corner, with nowhere to go.

No! I did not wait till it dried; it was gloss! That would have taken an eternity! I walked across the floor and

left my footprints too, as I escaped my manic mission.
Note to the world, I am banned from decorating
because I will paint anything in sight.

I set fire to the kitchen too because I left the stove chip
pan on while I was watching tv and then ran to my
sister's house to tell her my house was on fire instead of
ringing the fire brigade from my house phone in my
living room. Yup, definitely lacking in common sense!

I was associating with all the wrong people, people who
understood me though, misunderstood humans.
Alcoholics, glue sniffers and all those who come from a
life they want to hide from. I started hanging around
with this one guy in particular. He was addicted to
sniffing solvents and had nowhere to live. So, I offered
refuge at my flat as it was too big for just me.

The man became scary, and I was too afraid to tell him
to leave me alone. The icing on the cake though, was
when I visited Kent for a Christmas party at the
Howbury center. I loved the Christmas parties, there
was always a karaoke, so I would be on that all night
long.

However, upon returning to Gateshead, I got the fright of my life when I got home to find the man, I had so eagerly tried to evict sitting watching tv in my living room. I had previously retrieved my spare key from him, so I was confused at how he had got in.

Well! he broke in, he climbed up the drainpipe and in through the kitchen window. He knew I was away so squatted in my house. He then refused to leave, which involved me informing the police.

No longer feeling safe I decided to up and leave again, returning to Kent. I was then housed in a supported accommodation in Gravesend by the homeless department in Bexley Heath.

There was no support about it though. It was basically a three-bedroom house share with a shared lounge and kitchen. No support network, or service.

Well, actually, to be fair! I have a feeling the support was there, but nobody there to encourage and love me. That was until Liz and Pat moved in.

The couple took me under their wing, they loved me and cared for me like I was one of their own. I used to go on errands with them and eat with them, watch tv in the evenings with them. I was growing to love them. Do you remember me saying previously, that I was naïve? Well, get on this!

Every day, we would go shopping with Neil and Mel, a couple that were always around. Mel hated me for some reason and I never knew why. She always smoked this stuff on tin foil, and one day I asked her what it was. To which she replied it was just cannabis resin.

The issue was never raised again. After "Shopping" we would have to stop off at the chemist every day, to pick up Pat's prescription of methadone. Another thing I never questioned...

To top it off! One day I walked into the room and Liz was injecting something into Pat's arm, this I did question, and Liz replied that it was medicine and that he needed it, so he didn't get sick. I STILL did not cotton on.

Three of them were shoplifting, heroin addicts taking me on shoplifting missions and to score at seventeen years old. The new family I trusted were liars! That was not what made me leave though! Liz was a lot older than Pat and she was severely disabled.

Not to mention quite minted being on the high rate of DLA. Pat was a prolific drug user, criminal and in honesty he was just disgusting.

One day, we went out for a drive somewhere, just Pat and me. He offered to give me a driving lesson, and told me to climb between his legs, to reach the pedals.

Innocently I did so! He then began to try and kiss my neck, to which I almost drove into the tree. I asked him what he was doing? He responded telling me he loved me! I was mortified and told him to take me home.

Days later after a whole lot of awkwardness, I felt like I had betrayed Liz. She was the only decent one out of them. It was fairground season, and I had heard that there was a site not so far away.

So off I went with my troubles in my old kit bag and joined the fair again, only this time I travelled for a longer period of time.

Fairground life is really NOT!! As FUN as you would imagine. Yes, it is fun for those enjoying the rides, not fun for us building them up and pulling them down every few days.

It was a hard graft with no sex discrimination act in sight. I was treated like one of the men. Well, unless my boss Henry was hollering "Get your tit's out". When it came to work, I was one of the men.

We were doing a ground in Danson Park in Bexley heath, it was on the last day, when we were pulling down.

It was my first real experience of love at first sight. I was pulling down the juvenile and helping on the dodgems. Across the ground there was a guy called Marc who worked on the waltzer. I noticed him looking at me a few times and we had a little bit of banter as we crossed paths.

It was a brief encounter but I undoubtably felt a spark. Apparently, so did he.

To my delight, the next day, as we were building up on the new sight, I looked up to see Marc across the field. It turned out that he was going to be doing the next couple of grounds with us in Essex. In that time, we spent every spare moment together.

We fell in love like they do on a soppy romantic chick flick. Then at the end of the season we would spend all of our time in the trailer yard or down the local pub. I was totally head over heels in love with him! He was a good one.

When the new season began Marc and I were going to be separated for a couple of weeks, but we spoke every day on the phone. I longed to see him again, and I counted the days till it happened. If only he could have been so patient!

I was doing a ground in Blackheath, and Marc was in Tottenham, Henry was really getting on my nerves with his derogatory comments.

One day I told him to f-off and he sacked me. So, off I went to Tottenham to get a job with one of Marcs bosses. Whilst I was there, I discovered that Marc was actually cheating on me. So, hurting him more than him hurting me I decided to physically lay into him. I was like a lunatic punching him as he found the whole thing amusing.

I left the next day and never saw him again. Off up west feeling betrayed and alone, unsure of what I was going to do next. I can't remember how but somehow, I ended up in the lobby of the leaving care team. 300 miles away, back in Gateshead! Pleading for help.

Gateshead Social Services were less patient with me, than the Howbury center. They were evidently frustrated with me and sent me straight to the Civic Center to represent as homeless again. Having a strong connection in the area and being eighteen, the housing took on my case.

Another pause for thought! I was eighteen and still under a full care plan, struggling with poor mental health with high complex needs. Yet, when I was sent to the housing options service to represent as homeless, I had no accompanying support on either occasion...

I was referred back into the temporary hostel on Belle Vue bank, but after a short time I was placed into the local psychiatric unit in the Queen Elizabeth Hospital under a section. Which was when I attempted suicide, from taking an overdose of anti- depressant pills.

Chapter Four – Mentally Challenged

My very first suicide attempt was when I was about twelve or thirteen. I had been sent to an Indian family, which mortified me and there was nothing I could do. Let's just clarify I'm not a racist, something just didn't sit right with me living in this Muslim home.

I had been diagnosed with a urine infection and the Dr had prescribed me with a lot of pills, which I took all at once. I ended up in Greenwich hospital under the psychiatric care, to be assessed for my mental health.

Due to this attempt on my life, I went on to receive a new life label "mentally challenged" So, when I took a load of pills in the hostel at eighteen, I was automatically sectioned.

Admittedly I was young, very immature, and not to mention that the support I got in hospital made me feel safe. The hospital was right next to my dad's house too, so I would get constant visits from him.

To be honest, my dad is the only one who ever really cared. Unfortunately, because he was only my stepdad, my mum restricted the amount of help she would allow him to offer me. Not to mention the fact that he put up with so much hurt from me.

Whilst sectioned I went through some pretty intense therapy sessions, where I began to reveal my secrets. Then I would quickly close up again at the first sight of my demons from the past. Nobody could ever understand how my heart was shattered into so many pieces at such a young age.

How the secret of what that horrible woman did to me as a little girl had affected me. And the feelings of abandonment from the people that were supposed to love me no matter what.

The nurses would often find me sleeping under my bed, not understanding why. They just labeled me depressed and anxious. Nobody had any idea what I saw in my dreams, the things that hurt me and scared me. I wasn't just depressed, I was traumatized.

After spending six or more weeks in the tranwell unit and some sofa surfing at my dad's house, I finally got a new one bedroom flat in Felling, Gateshead. It was a ten-minute walk from my dad's house, it was perfect.

After a short time of mixing with the wrong people though, I found myself pregnant as a result of a one-night stand.

Wow! Finally! I was going to have unconditional love. Sadly, it was short lived due to a miscarriage at twelve weeks. So, you know that tolerance to pain I mentioned earlier? This devastated me! I wanted to be a mum so bad.

I still had to go for my 12 weeks scan, I remember the day like it was yesterday, my social worker took me to the QE because I had been bleeding a few days before. She stayed with me during the scan to make sure all was okay. The doctor confirmed that I had lost the baby through a miscarriage. My social worker held my hand as I sobbed...

Losing the baby, sent me spiraling out of control, I have never really been able to handle painful emotions well.

So, whenever I felt hurt, I would bottle it up and mask it with substance abuse and crazy behavior.

Not long after I got my flat, my mum moved up to the North East too because she had split up with her partner. My dad allowed her to stay in the spare room, but she took advantage of my dad, and had a breakdown and ended up in the psychiatric unit herself. I can't quite remember all the details, but somehow, she was sectioned.

Whilst she was in hospital, I would visit her every day, and we actually grew quite close. We have periods where we can be so loving towards each other, then bam world war three kicks off.

When my mum was discharged from hospital, she was given a two-bedroom flat in the Centre of Gateshead. Despite a few hurdles we grew closer and became more and more excited as Christmas got closer.

Although we were both skint and only had a meal and a spliff between us, it was a nice Christmas. We were spending it together for the first time, in a long time so I was happy with that.

Over the festive period, mum had received contact from an old friend in Lewisham.
He was staying at a pub that needed staff for New Year's Eve and my mum being a licensed pub manager she jumped at the chance.

When my mum informed me of her plan to go to London for a couple of days, I jumped straight on the band wagon.

London, for New Years, I'll have some of that! I had it all mapped out in my head, I would get there and spend the night begging on the strand in my old pitch.

Within a few days, once the social book was cashed, and the tickets were paid for. There was me and mum on the late coach to London. Both of us excited in our own way. Mum was going to work in a pub, and I was going up west to see my old friends #Reunion.

I arrived up west and headed straight for the Strand, it was late in the afternoon by now, I'd spent most of the day with my mum at the pub she was going to be working in. When I arrived on the Strand, I was delighted to see my street brother Ben, a few years younger than me, I used to call him my little brother.

He was sat with two other men, Andy and Paul who were brothers from Peterlee near Durham. Speaking broad Geordie, I sparked the interest of the elder brother Paul, who was thirty-six years old.

Andy was much younger than his brother, he was around twenty.

After some long conversations and time with Paul, I became quite fond of him and the next thing I knew we were kissing. Not something that I usually do, kiss a stranger! Something was in his eyes though. Something that made me want to love him, care for him, and save him.

****

Sitting reflecting on the coach as me and mum pulled out of London Victoria Station, returning home from our very brief trip. I realized that I had to come back soon. I could come back to London, pick him up and take him back to my flat in felling. That is exactly what happened.

Not even two days later, mum and I were making the same trip to London, only mum wasn't coming back, and Paul was instead.

Forty-eight hours later I'm back behind the theatre at St. Martin's in the field, collecting the man I thought I was destined to save. To my horror as I approached the place he slept. I found him coming out of a red phone box with a needle hanging from his groin.

This didn't put me off in the slightest, I still thought I could save him. As weeks past in Newcastle, Paul became sly and would use behind my back at every opportunity.

Finding out I was pregnant, didn't stop him either. Six weeks into the pregnancy, he decided enough was enough. He cashed his giro, left me standing on the street corner as he dashed for the coach station.

I was devastated! how dare he! I couldn't believe this no-good waste of space had left me and his unborn child, to go and be with his first love heroin.

After around half an hour waiting on the corner of felling high street, I decided to take a trip to the social services. I hadn't yet informed them of my current predicament, so found this a great opportunity to do so.

I told my social worker all about the pregnancy, and how Paul had just abandoned me. I went on to tell her that my mum was still in London and that I wanted to go and see her and tell her I was pregnant.

A travel warrant was issued, and I jumped on the 3pm train getting me into Charing Cross around 7pm. When I arrived, I couldn't wait to tell everybody of this horrible turn of events.

Andy especially was mortified at his big brothers' behavior. I was curious as to why Paul hadn't come back to Charing cross, surely, he would have no choice?

The next morning, I was awoken by a whisper "Andy, psst Andy" I jumped up to find Paul standing there looking back in sheer horror. The look of how is she here? It's actually quite comical to be fair, looking back on the moment.

After a week or so chasing the drugs in London, Paul chose to return to Newcastle with me to make a proper go of it. Just the three of us.

Chapter Five – Addicted

I lost my flat in felling due to abandonment, whilst I was chasing Paul down in London. So, we ended up moving into my mums two bedroom flat in Gateshead high street. She was staying in London, and it made it easier for her, if we were in the flat so that the council didn't twig that nobody was there.

The only trouble is, it was the same block of flats as Paul's heroin dealer lived in so, he was back on the gear and hammering it. Every night we would head over to the key side in Newcastle and I would sit and beg outside the slug and lettuce pub, while Paul kept a look out for the police.

Fun fact: it is illegal to beg and it is an arrestable offence, so we had to be vigilant. I made a fortune begging because I was so young looking, and my bump was growing into view. Easy money to pay for Paul's addiction.

One night while I was begging, a lady that I recognized stopped at my begging spot. I was mortified because it was someone that worked with my social worker.

Which obviously got back to the office. I was already being assessed on my ability to parent my unborn child and here I was begging for heroin (not even for me!) on a cold evening whilst pregnant.

My unborn son was placed on the child protection register, because I was "Out of control" I was nineteen and very troubled, it felt like everyone around me was expecting me to fail. Being the people pleaser that I was, that's exactly what I did, fail!

Social services had no faith in me, the support was not there in fact it was like a tag team against me. The first time I met the baby's social worker, she informed me that they would be taking my baby. That was very early on in the pregnancy, they wanted my baby and were going to do anything to get it, even lie in a child protection meeting...

I was about six months gone and we had to attend a meeting at Gateshead library. The meeting was a normal for me having been under social services since I was ten. The meeting was to decide on my son staying on the child protection register.

There was about twelve people in the room and only one of them on my side that was the baby's dad. My social worker was there, supposed to be a support for me, instead she assassinated my character, claiming I was too unstable and that I was so unhinged that I had lied about being pregnant a year before...

Wait a minute! Pause for thought...

This was the same social worker that held my hand, whilst I lay on the bed, sobbing because the sonographer had just told me I had in fact had a miscarriage! Yet here she is sat in a child protection meeting saying I made the whole thing up. Somebody please kindly remove the knife from my back.
I was like a bull and she was the red flag, I exploded! Proving her right, I was unhinged, but c'mon that was a shallow move.

After all of the exposure to heroin that I had witnessed, it finally got me. I was nineteen and pregnant. Growing more and more curious, I asked Paul what was the deal with this drug? He said, it takes your cares away and it's just like smoking a joint.

He offered me some on the foil, I had nothing to lose. I had already been informed that my child was being removed from my care by the local authority due to my chaotic history. Meaning that I was too unstable and unsettled to be able to parent my unborn child.

Basically "written off."

This fact destroyed me, yes, I was unsettled, but all I ever wanted to be was a mum, to feel unconditional love. Instead, that was being ripped away from me by the local authority because they apparently knew best.

All I ever needed was someone to believe in me. Encourage me and nurture me not completely write me off.

I became addicted very quickly and our habit grew larger as the two of us were now using at least three bags each a day. We became homeless when my mum kicked us out, Paul had turned her house into a smack den, so she told us to leave when she moved back from London to save her flat.

At first at first, I was put back into Bell Vue hostel on my own, but then Paul and I got placed in a bed and breakfast in Whitley Bay together when a room became available. It was a matter of days before we were asked to leave the little bed and breakfast though, and we were forced to sleep on the streets.

With all options and resources being exhausted, there was little we could do. I didn't want to ask social services for help, they were taking my baby, I didn't trust them as far as I could throw them.

Here we were! addicted, pregnant, and homeless. As the habit grew bigger, along with my bump, we became more noticeable in the shops we were stealing from to buy our gear.

We were becoming sloppy and cocky which inevitably led to our arrest. It was my first adult offence, so I got away with a caution, Paul on the other hand was a known criminal so was immediately remanded into custody. I was devastated, with no clue as to what I was going to do.

Here I was, all alone, no place to call home. I made my way to a mutual friend's house; I knew she could help me get out of trouble. She had given me some gear and some sound advice.

She then helped me get somewhere to stay in an area that was alien to me. I only stayed there two days as I slowly detoxed on some subitex the girl had given me.

Feeling devastated at the consequences of my actions, it was time to eat an enormous amount of humble pie. I made way to Gateshead leaving care team to beg them for help, no longer caring about trust issues. The time had come for me to get my act together, my unborn son was owed much more than what he was already receiving.

When I explained all to Alison, my social worker at the time, she was deeply concerned for the wellbeing of my child. She made some calls, and I was admitted into the Queen Elizabeth Hospital onto the pre-natal ward. I was to remain there until the baby was born.

During my stay at the Queen Elizabeth, I was determined to break free from heroin, and my recovery was on track. It was as if I was living in some fantasy bubble. Paul would be released any day; he would be clean from his forced prison detox. I had been clean two weeks from my hospital detox, it was a winner, winner chicken dinner scenario.

If only the same scenario could have existed in Paul's head! As soon as he got out, the first thing he said to me, was shall we go and score?! That was the first relapse. Temptation waved under my nose for the first time in sixteen day's and I caved! What an idiot! I was so blinded by love, it was a pretend love, but it was love all the same.

All my hard work was undone by that one fix! Paul didn't care that we had just managed a sixteen-day detox, he had no intention of getting clean. I was still determined though!

It was around six weeks between Paul's release and the birth of our son. Jack Paul was born on Tuesday 5th October weighing 6lb 9oz. Becoming a mother was the most magical moment of my life, looking down at my perfect little boy. The hatred I had felt towards the world for so many years, replaced with unconditional love. The joy was short lived though; I was only going to be this beautiful baby boys' mother for a matter of days.

*****

It was around twenty-four hours before the headache really kicked in. I had been moved to a side room due to my special circumstances shall we say. I'd been getting mild headaches which the doctors were reluctant to treat, due to my previous opiate addiction. Then! The headaches just hit me like a wrecking ball.

Due to the epidural piercing a hole in my spine, spinal fluids were leaking to my brain. This is what was causing the headaches, and extreme discomfort.

The only way to treat this rare issue, was to do a spinal procedure to inject blood into the hole. The procedure didn't work the first time, so it had to be done twice. The headaches were so unbearable and the pain in my spine was of the same, I was crippled!

Despite being in all this pain I was still not giving in; I wasn't going to take the one pure painkiller that Paul was willing to prescribe.

It didn't stop him using though! He would have a hit in the toilet when he visited us in the hospital. Jack had been moved to special care to be monitored for methadone withdrawal and because I was in no fit state to care for him.

One day, the nurses were in my room doing my observations. They found a needle with some liquid in it and asked me what it was. Completely stunned as I had no idea it was there, I replied with "what does it look like" in my defense I was also high on codeine, that the doctor had finally prescribed me.

Not able to completely comprehend the situation, upon further questioning I took the blame for the needle. One of those moments where I look back in my life and literally just want to punch myself in the face. To my complete shock I was arrested, and Paul was nowhere to be seen.

Still in agony from my epidural crisis, I was escorted off of the hospital premises by the police. Arrested for possession, the police took me to the custody suite at Gateshead police station. I must have zonked out on the meds as soon as my head hit the rubber pillow!

I was awoken by a guard, he called me out to be charged with the crime. Still hobbling, with my head down in pain I slowly walked to the desk sergeant. I was being released with a caution, it was a minor charge, with no need for further action.

Released in the cold, on a night in early October with no place to go. I was in the same pajamas that I had been wearing for four or five days. They were soiled with blood and I hadn't showered!

My dignity was lost and so was my parental responsibility. Due to this turn of events, there was no way social services were going to allow me to have any rights to Jack.

Totally devastated, I made way to a place behind the high street where Paul and I used to sleep. To my amazement, when I arrived there, I found Paul bedding down.

I was completely overwhelmed! Distraught by the consequences of my actions, I just needed a cuddle. I didn't care that he had hidden and watched throughout the whole ordeal of me being arrested.

Discharged from hospital due to a possession charge, I was not allowed to visit Jack without security present. Something that was meant to be magical, was turned into something so shameful. The social services had won a court order, and Jack was discharged into their care.

The next two months were unbearable, the constant battles, and my grandfather dying. I became too weak to fight anymore and my addiction was back and stronger than ever.
It was Christmas time 2004, Jack's first Christmas. I knew it was going to be tough, celebrating without him so I just took enough gear to block it all out. Or I cried myself to sleep, because I couldn't nurse my crying baby, because someone else was.

I had never felt such pain, and it wasn't going away.

Paul and I decided we needed to get away, so we chose to return to London. Despite not having anywhere to go, we didn't care it had to be better than where we were. Jack was being looked after, and we weren't going away for long.

So, we thought! We actually never came back!

We landed in London Victoria around 6am in the morning, we got the late coach and slept the whole way from Newcastle to London. As soon as we arrived, we headed straight to score, we had no worries just freedom.

A pocket full of cash and a habit to feed, we wandered around Tottenham court road to find an early morning shotter. When we finally scored, we scored some crack too. Paul put the heroin and crack together to create a snowball.

The max effect! The buzz was so euphoric, I was hooked on the first hit. Unaware at the time how addictive this new combination was, it wasn't long before I was completely addicted, and we were taking hundreds of pounds worth a day.

Early 2005 we were officially, street homeless in Piccadilly. Taking £60 worth of snowballs every two hours. The pain was no longer existent, and the thoughts of losing my son were a memory now stored away.

All that motivated me was my next fix, begging was profitable for me because of my fresh face and sad eyes. As the habit grew larger though, so did our confidence to shoplift again.

As time went on, I began to resent Paul, he was like a leech. He'd be up my bum if I was providing the money, soon as I wasn't making any I was beaten and spat on.

Crack and heroin are like an evil spirit, possessing anyone who consumes it.

Now, would be a good time to point out although I may be a big softy at heart, I took no rubbish from anyone! So, if I got hit, he was getting hit back. For around a year we slept in the back doorway of Waterstones on Jermyn Street in Piccadilly. Living each day as it came, taking drugs was our only motivation.

It was around a year after we landed in London, I remember because it was snowing hard and the street outreach workers were on our case to get in somewhere. There had apparently been an urgent weather warning over the snow and shelters were rolling out all over London.

Completely freezing and desperate for some warmth and decent food we caved and decided to get off of the streets and into the St' Mungo's rolling shelter in Marylebone.

It was literally a bed, we didn't care to engage, both myself and Paul were completely anti service. Personally, I had engaged with services pretty much all my life and they kept letting me down, so at this point I didn't trust them as far as I could throw them.

When we moved into the rolling shelter, despite the disengagement with services, we became comfortable in the setting. We would beg all day to feed our habits, then chill indoors of an evening watching TV.

Around six weeks after moving into the rolling shelter, a couple's room became available in a hostel on the outskirts of Westminster, near Holborn. That was when we had moved into another St. Mungo's hostel on Endel Street.

The hostel had an in-house substance misuse clinic, and a support team in every area of need. I personally took advantage and got myself on a methadone script. Crack was my drug of choice now, heroin just held me back with the sickness that came along with it.

My love for drugs had removed any glimmer of thought for anything or anyone else.
Paul was sent to prison on a warrant, which was my get out of jail free card.

Now Paul was out of my way, there was no stopping me! I would shoplift all day, selling my stuff to the brasses, in the flats on Wardour Street. From perfumes to Radley handbags, I was on a mission. I would graft on Oxford Street, sell on Wardour Street and score on Dean Street all within an hour. I was on fire, and cocky with it!

The trouble is when you become invisible in your mind, from the crack. The more noticeable you are to the world around you.

After a short time, I was back on the streets, all alone on Piccadilly. The failure to keep to my tenancy agreement and the constant crack use had got me kicked out of the hostel. More for my attitude whilst being under the influence rather than being on the substance itself.

I was gutted because I did like living at Endel street, the in-house services were convenient. However, I was smack bang in the middle of temptation, which always won against the odds in terms of recovery. I wasn't ready to sort it out! I didn't want to face my past, I wanted to forget it!

In 2006 I began sleeping rough alone on Piccadilly opposite Fortnum and Mason, you could say the richest strip in London. Starting at Piccadilly Circus and ending in Green Park, Mayfair. I felt safe, because it was a secure, highly patrolled area.

I had become isolated in my own little world, numb from the pain which was being blocked out with my extreme drug intake. Nobody liked me, I was always upsetting people. I had no respect for anyone or anything.

I would leave my belongings where I woke, to go and score. Nine times out of ten, I would come back to find them gone. Either taken by other homeless people or binned by the street cleaners. It was either pack everything I own into a backpack and carry it around all day, or risk leaving it.

Personally, I was always a risk taker choosing to leave my belongings over the physical back and shoulder pain from carrying my stuff everywhere. All I cared about was my next pipe! There was no room in my life to risk any more psychological pain.

Completely dis-engaged with services, I wasted away on the pavements in Piccadilly. Whenever outreach workers would wake me, I would tell them to f-off and leave me alone. I was so tired of the repetitive cycle of trying to get in somewhere.

Every time I engaged with a homeless service or hostel, I would have to have a "Key work evaluation" which involved me continuously going over my life events, something I was desperate to forget, hence the hundreds of pounds worth of drugs a day.

"Do these people, not know how to save a file?" Or "do these services even communicate?"
Would be my thought process! No! It was easier to disengage. If it is just me in my world, then nobody can hurt me.

Chapter Six – Arrested

It was Christmas week 2006, I was begging in my usual spot at the Alliance and Leicester on Piccadilly. The money people gave at Christmas time was unreal. It would take me about twenty minutes to make twenty pounds, it was like a pound a minute. Unfortunately, along with the rise in generosity, came a rise in police patrol.

I was just casually sitting, not even being volatile, when a car pulls up. Two plain clothes officers jump out of the car, all dramatic and nick me on the spot. Before I could blink, I was standing in custody, being read my rights.

Pulling out the mental health card, I pleaded suicidal, which led to me being released without charge into the care of the Westminster Psychiatric Unit on a 48hr section for an assessment.

Well, psychotic was an understatement! I wanted out, from the minute I arrived. The ward was run by very large, hospital staff nurses.

Most were African and didn't take no crap from anyone. I really was a weed compared to them! It didn't stop me coming up against them though. A mixture of men and women but equal in strength all the same.

I made way for the door on many occasions within the next 48hrs, without success. It was the most excruciating time of my life! I was forced to have a shower by the women, when I say forced, I mean forced! Pinned down, fully clothed scrubbed with shampoo and very lukewarm water.

I kicked off like a wild animal which resulted in me getting a large shot of chlorpromazine in my backside that instantly knocked me out. When it finally wore off, I was free to go...

Still in a haze from the chlorpromazine and looking like a scarecrow I made my way up west. The hospital was only in Victoria, so I just jumped on the 453 bus to Piccadilly and jumped off at the Haymarket.

I wasn't bothered about scoring, not only did the doctors pump me with mood altering drugs, but they also pumped me full of substance blocking drug, naltrexone.

I actually had no cravings it was some pretty good stuff. Instead of hunting down a fix, I went on a hunt for JP. It was Christmas eve and this year, all I wanted for Christmas was to be JP's girl. (I don't want to use his name so I'm going to call him JP)

JP and I met, whilst I was still with Paul. There was an instant spark, but I always stayed faithful to Paul, even though I always knew that JP would treat me better.

JP would always tell me how beautiful I was and how if I was his girl, he would treat me like a princess. I can't deny, although I was faithful, I longed for a day that I could be JP's girl. When I finally left Paul, I just wasn't interested in being tied down with someone else.

I did spend time with JP, and we did grow closer, but we were too far into the friend's zone, it felt weird to go beyond that now. Until this happened...

It wasn't too long before I found him on the corner of Endel Street. His eyes lit up as I walked towards him. He was on his push bike; it was kind of his getaway vehicle. I stopped in front of him and asked him what he wanted for Christmas. To which he replied "you".

I looked back and said to him, "well you have got me!". We went back to his hostel where I stayed for a few days. We had to sneak me in and out though because I wasn't supposed to be there. But it was the most magical few days of my life.

I was totally in love and felt like a princess. Listening intently as he showered me with soft words of affirmation. The relationship, however, began with a rocky start, from our turbulent personality's but we finally got together properly after a brief stint of him being in prison.

Whilst JP was inside, I had got into a Look Ahead hostel in Bayswater, London. I was only in there a few days before JP was released. When he got out, he was so proud to call me his girl.

I was clean most day's but JP and me would binge on crack at the weekends.

We had the most romantic summer that year, going on bike rides through Hyde park, having food by the duck pond. it was perfection.

After the honeymoon period though, crack became our number one priority and once again the addiction became more to me than life itself. JP and I were like bonnie and Clyde we got on so well one minute, in the blink of an eye we would be trying to kill each other.

There would be periods of time that we would be stuck to each other like glue, then other times it was like we were not even together. I was with JP two years, then he became psychotic, trying to tie me up and strangle me or he would lock me in a flat, insisting he would kill me if I left him.

One day I was begging outside the Sainsbury's local on Tottenham Court Road, JP hated it when I begged, and I knew word would get back to him that I was begging there.

Unfortunately for me, the police were also alerted that I was begging outside the store. Arrested on a warrant, I was remanded in custody and sent to Holloway prison. It wasn't my first time inside; it was my second.

The warrant was for a common assault on a community support officer. The officer had antagonized me whilst trying to move me on. I was sleeping outside the Alliance and Leicester on Piccadilly; it was my favorite spot because it was sheltered.

Personally, I slept like a baby no matter where I slept, I used my rucksack or coat as a pillow and sometimes I had a blanket or sleeping bag. One morning two community support officers stopped, tried to wake me, and move me on. I love my sleep!! So, I didn't wake instantly, so then the officer decided to kick the bag under my head instead.

I jumped up and got fired up, he was provoking me by telling me he was going to arrest me!

For what? Sleeping! Why kick my "Pillow" with your size ten steel toe cap? I got so angry and obviously can't physically kick him to see how he liked it, so I spat at him. I was sentenced to six weeks in prison, which I would only serve three weeks of, as most charges are halved in time.

My second time in Holloway was more enlightening than the first time.

The time before this one was for a begging charge; I was only in Holloway for the weekend and slept right through it. This time I was in for three weeks so I would say it was the most educational out of the two trips to the prison.

Heading straight to the detox wing once the booking in process had finished, it felt more like a hospital ward. With cells ranging from four beds, two beds or single cells.

Sharing a cell was last on my list of priorities, there was no way! If only I had a choice. I was put in a four-bed cell with three other ladies. Two of the ladies were lovers and made no secret of it and another was due to be released.

Don't get me wrong they were lovely ladies; I just couldn't handle the social interaction 24 hours a day. I thrived on isolation not integration.

The time went by quickly, and the next thing I knew I was released. Pleading that I would never be going to prison again, I found myself back in the middle of SoHo searching for JP, whom I hadn't heard from the past three weeks I had been inside.

I was gutted to hear later that day that JP too had been arrested and was now serving time in Pentonville Prison. Whilst JP was inside for around ten weeks, I was chaotic. Staying awake for days on end smoking crack and cranking up my grafting methods. I had discovered clipping!

Clipping is where a guy thinks he's paying for sex, yet the girl takes the money and runs. Well, my young fresh face brought me many client's and lots of money. I would go days without stopping, I was in a world of my own.

Due to my extreme crack addiction, I would need some heroin to bring me back down, so it wasn't long before I was back on the gear again too...

I was back sleeping rough in Piccadilly, London. I had been on a five-day crack binge and needed to stop and take a timeout. Crack was my only motivation, I had nothing to live for in the Groundhog Day that became my life. It was like I was lost in a world that I so desperately wanted to escape. A world that was driven by drugs and crime.

A life that is not worthy of human habitation.

Chapter Seven – I Want to Break Free

On this night in particular I was bedding down outside the embassy opposite the Christopher Wren Church on Piccadilly. I slept there a lot when I was on a comedown from the crack, it always felt much safer for some unknown reason. I had no blankets, so I huddled in a ball facing the doorway of the Maltease Embassy.

I remember hearing a whisper it said "Kerri, come on I've chosen you" thinking I was hallucinating, I just ignored it. Feeling a little claustrophobic from being so close to the door, I turned, opened my eyes in the restlessness and I saw what looked like a silhouette of a man sitting on the roof on the Christopher Wren church. I was definitely tripping, right?

I had been hammering the crack for days without even stopping for food. No way, I was either dreaming or tripping there is absolutely no other explanation.

A few days later I was begging at the TSB cashpoint next door to the embassy, it was early in the evening and it had just turned dark.

Looking up to ask someone for change, I was shocked to see my boyfriend JP standing in front of me. He was fuming at me, he'd just been released from prison, where I abandoned him for my first love crack.

Now, he's here and I'm sat disrespecting him by begging. Boy did the proverbial hit the fan. After some harsh explicit language, and some saliva in my face, then off he went on his own mission of self-destruct.

Given the fact I had just got off lightly, in terms of JP's wrath it was safe to say, my best bet now was to stay well away from Soho. It must have been around 7pm because I remember thinking that it was about the time that the soup run goes to the strand.

Ever since I was thirteen, I have always found myself retreating to the Strand to where I spent most of my teenage years. There would always be an elder there, someone who treated me like their little sister, or sometimes I'd have a street uncle.

It would be one of the older, longer standing homeless men, always a man though and often over-protective.

I guess thinking about it I just always needed a dominant male influence in my life. My daddy issues may also have a part to play in that too from a psychological perspective.

When I arrived at the strand there was already about three or four vans parked up.

One for food, one for clothes, one for blankets and sleeping bags, then there would be one for transporting the volunteers. They were all religious people from different churches, doing their duty of goodwill, I liked the Irish gypsy's the best though, those are the ones I felt most drawn to. Feeling pretty sorry for myself, I attempted to just get my soup, sandwich and blankets and then do one.

The gypsies on the other hand wanted to stop and chat. Not really feeling the need for any idol chit chat, but ignorant I am not, so, I stopped to talk. The conversation, went a little something like this...

I highlight the word "Something like", please do not quote me on the actual conversation."

Gypsy Man 1: Hi, how are you, we haven't seen you in a while, you know you are welcome to come to our church, in Swanley.

Me: Yeah, I'm good thanks, erm yeah okay my best friend Ann lives in Swanley maybe next time I visit her.

Gypsy Man 1: Okay, well we have a minibus that comes to the car park at Charing Cross station, every Sunday to collect you guys so you are always welcome.

Me: Okay, thanks maybe I'll **stop** by one day.

Gypsy Man 2: Do you believe Kerri?

Me: Yeah, I believe in God

Gypsy Man 2: Do you believe in Jesus.

Me: I guess so He's the son of God, isn't he?

Gypsy Man 2: Yes, have you ever accepted Jesus Kerri?

Me: What do you mean?

Gypsy Man 2: Have you ever said a prayer inviting Jesus as your lord and savior?

Me: No!

Gypsy Man 2: Would you like to?

Me: Yeah okay... I guess I had nothing to lose.

Then the Gypsy Man asked me to repeat the words after him. They went a little something like this...

Dear God, I know that I am a sinner and there is nothing that I can do to save myself. I confess my complete helplessness to forgive my own sin or to work my way to heaven. At this moment I trust Christ alone as the One who bore my sin when He died on the cross. I believe that He did all that will ever be necessary for me to stand in your holy presence. I thank you that Christ was raised from the dead as a guarantee of my own resurrection. As best as I can, I now transfer my trust to Him. I am grateful that He has promised to receive me despite my many sins and failures. Father, I take you at your word. I thank you that I can face death now that you are my Savior. Thank you for the assurance that you will walk with me through the deep valley. Thank you for hearing this prayer. In Jesus' Name. Amen.

After declaring the prayer, I wrapped up the conversation to avoid any brain washing attempts and made a swift exit. All filled up from my soup and sandwich, I made way back to Piccadilly to get my head down. I really couldn't be bothered with any drama, something that was inevitable if I stepped foot in Soho.

Not long after I settled down in my usual pitch at the Alliance and Leicester opposite Fortnum and Mason, I got a twenty-pound drop and it burnt a hole straight through my blanket. The urge and temptation for crack, overcame the fear of bumping into JP. The next thing I knew I was standing at the top of Wardour Street scoring two rocks.

Trying my best to go un-noticed I hurried to a secret smoking spot I used to go to on other side of oxford street. I had a secret space because I needed it.

I was so giving, even as a raging junky I was always giving my drugs away through lack of greed. I must have been the only person, to give a beggar my last pound to buy what they needed to get them through their pain. All in it together I used to say, ha, now I say sleep with one eye open in that world.

After my little session in my secret place across the other side of Oxford Street, I made way back to my pitch to call it a night. Having no idea just what had actually occurred. No idea of what door I had just opened.

I must have slept for sixteen hours solid because when I woke a whole day was missing, the day had already slipped away.

Instead of waking to commuters going to work, I was greeting them going home. Bonus! My cup was full, and I had made enough to score my first eye opener. Someone had kindly left some food too which I scoffed on the way to score.

It was around 5pm so it was rush hour, not just rush hour for workers but also rush hour for scoring too. There were shotters but they were scarce, avoiding getting "Rushed" by the police. The only thing is, when dealers go into hiding there ends up being a big huddle of drug addicts in the middle of Shaftsbury avenue desperate to score.

This day in particular, one of those desperate drug addicts was JP. He had been on a proper blowout since his release from prison and was strung out for a pipe.

As soon as he saw me it was like a red flag to the bull. He made his way towards me, to what I thought was a reconciliation maybe, turned into me getting sparked right in the mouth which led to an instant fat lip, then off he rode on his bike down the middle of China Town.

He must have done a left on to Shaftsbury Avenue because he was back within minutes. The shotter had just turned up as he hit me, so he did a circle around the block, picked up his crack and disappeared.

Scurrying off in the opposite direction, I made way to the back of Jermyn Street in Piccadilly to smoke the drugs I had just purchased.

Days past and weeks too, all in which time I grew tired of the hamster wheel I was living on. JP and I were hanging on by a thread, there was no value to our lives let alone relationship.

One night, sitting crouched on the floor outside the embassy, feeling defeated and depressed, I Looked up at the church in front of me and began to sob uncontrollably.

I cried and cried till I couldn't cry anymore, pleading "if God was real, why am I living this way" going on to say, "God if you are real get me out of this now!"

I had hit rock bottom, I needed out. Surely there was no more this life could throw at me. I was twenty-three with no life ahead of me, surely this wasn't my destiny. Was it?

After that night, I began to feel stronger, more able to bounce back from whatever was upsetting me from the night before. Allowing my inner strength to surface I began mentally equipping myself for the fight.

With this new-found determination I was able to think more clearly, find logic within my current circumstance, the sort of logic as to why am I here exactly? With this thought in mind, I decided it was time to get off of the streets. Withdrawing from heroin, I made way to Look Ahead Bayswater, a hostel I stayed in previously.

I had been evicted because, I threw a tantrum and called one of the lady staff a female dog. I had an argument with JP, and it got heated, when the staff member tried to intervene, I told her where to go which ended in my eviction. It didn't help my case that she was the manager of the project.

Here I was though, making my way there, not quite sure what was going to happen when I got there. I knew you had to be referred in but that did not stop me.

When I first arrived, I asked to see the lady who I thought was the manager, to be informed that she was no longer there. I asked if I could see the new manager instead, to my joy it was Tom, someone who I got on quite well with in L.A Bayswater.

Tom called me into his office and informed me that I knew the process of referrals. Pleading with him that I just wanted help, and it was too long going through the process of representing at a day center first to then get referred into the next available hostel. It wasn't long before Tom responded with "let me see what I can do".

Within a couple of hours, I was moved back in, somehow, I had found favor and fortunately for me my old room was empty. This was a blessing, my prayers were being answered, I was breaking free.

L.A Bayswater is actually the nicest, homeliest hostel I ever lived in. It had more of a children's home feel to it. The staff there were so supportive, they would attend every appointment with you in the rehabilitation process. I was ready to take advantage of every aspect of that service.

I had no belongings with me, just a chicken and mushroom pot noodle that I had robbed from the Tesco on Bayswater road. I had no intention of using, I wanted out! I withdrew from heroin for the next twenty-four hours, cold turkey. It was the worst sickness I have ever been subject to. Cold sweats, hot flushes, stomach cramps and restlessness and so on.

I spent the whole night in the tv room watching movies on Sky.

I attended the doctor's the next day and was referred to S.R.A.C. A drug dependency clinic run by the NHS. I was prescribed methadone and allocated a keyworker through the rehabilitation center the Hungerford Drug Project.

One week past, then another week, the methadone kicked in properly and I was rearing for clean life. I felt so in control of my life, for the first time ever, I was dreaming of a better life. JP was in prison again and we weren't talking, in fact I had completely forgotten about him in terms of any romance or emotional attachment.

No! Nothing could hold me back now!

Not one thing.

Chapter Eight – Live or Die

Feeling fresh and looking for purpose, I started to attend the Hungerford Drug Project drop-in on Wardour Street.

Okay, Wardour Street is kind of shotters galore, but I was determined, and this was a huge test to that determination. I was not backing down. There would be all sorts of services available to make you feel more human and opportunities to enhance your learning.

Some days there would be I.T training or photography, my favorite was sound engineering. There would always be lunch club followed with some kind of alternative therapy. Acupuncture was the one I found the most beneficial, it would relax me into a space of complete serenity. I would become so relaxed; it would put me to sleep.

Part of the service was a blood Bourne virus clinic, Fiona from S.R.A.C would come in every Wednesday to do blood testing for intravenous related virus's such as

Hepatitis and HIV. With nothing to lose, I decided to get tested.

Within a week of being tested, I was called in to Fiona's office, where she gave me a full house on the diagnoses. I'd caught all three! What had I done, I had signed my own death warrant with my chaotic behavior, this was something that could not be fixed?

Completely distraught at the consequences of my own action's there was only one thing that could ease my pain, I needed a pipe and I needed it quick. I had so many thoughts in my head, screaming what have you done, what are you going to tell JP? You have to tell him; he could have it too!

The only thing that was going to shut up the voices was a big fat pipe.

One pipe turned in to two, then three and then the next thing I knew I was on a four-day bender. Then when I was finally ready to face the music, I went back to the hostel. Only to find out that JP had been looking for me. What?! JP is out?

Yes, JP was out and on the war path again because I had once again abandoned him while he was inside. I really didn't need his selfish insecurities right now. I just made way to my bedroom to bed.

A couple of hours later I was called by the staff, JP was at the door and I needed to sign him in, really!!? What did he want?

I guessed that this would be the perfect opportunity to tell him. Blaming it on a sexual assault that took place the last time I lived in the hostel, it was brushed under the carpet as a not my fault kind of issue.

It was my fault though wasn't it. I was a dirty little smack head, and this was my own doing. I use the term smack head because that was the label society gave me, not because it is how I look at homeless drug addicts. Or myself anymore!

Inevitably, this was a massive set back in my recovery, I was going to die, I was a ticking time bomb, my life as I knew it was over. This was the nail to the coffin for sure. So much for making a clean break! This life had to have some kind of vendetta against me. Smoking continuously again I lost all control; it was a live or die mentality...

With this new revelation, came hurricane Kerri! I was a whirlwind of emotion and JP was Jekyll and Hyde, blowing hot and cold from one minute to the next.

I got into trouble at look ahead Bayswater, so, I was moved into the last chance saloon of hostels. Look Ahead Victoria. L.A Victoria was one of the most notorious hostels in Westminster it was more like a legalized crack den. If you wanted any gear, you just had to rock up at Look Ahead Victoria, and you would be sorted.

Recovery in a place like this hostel was not going to be done easily.

It had been around six weeks since my diagnosis and I was growing tired of the constant crack binging. I was body popping for five days solid, dropping for twenty-four hours, to then get up to do it all again.

Something within me, so desperately wanted to change, but for what? What did I have that was worth fighting for? Then one day, clear as a bell, I heard a voice in my head, I heard these words...

"If you don't get your act together, you will be dead in two years and will never see Jack again."

It was so distinct, so powerful!

Once again, I would try recovery, I can so do this, I thought to myself. JP and I were evidently over, we were hanging on to each other by a thread, but it was over.

Although Look Ahead Victoria was notoriously known for its reputation of substance abusers, the support was bang on and it was available 24-7. When I think of this hostel, its strange because, it really was bad!

The staff though! They were something different. At first, I had my walls up, I kept myself to myself, not really engaging with anyone other than the receptionist for my post.

One day I lost it, I can't remember the details specifically, but I was ready to harm myself, and the key workers were at my door. I think I was extremely intoxicated this day, feeling sorry for myself and the reality of my circumstances, I wanted to die.

Glimpsing back, I remember sliding down the door sobbing because I couldn't take any more! I was barely an adult and my life were pretty much over already.

Little did I know but Kathleen, one of the keyworkers! Was on the other side of the door crying for me. A fact I never knew till recently, but to point out the compassion is important!

After that day Kath and Lucy my two keyworkers, gradually broke down the walls and I was finally ready to engage. I had also attended court for a crime and was given a conditional discharge, so I had to be on my best behavior. I was ready to do this!

I was living in the women's block of the hostel; and I'd just started to settle in and take advantage of the rehabilitation services they offered. I was looking forward to doing the military fitness in particular, because apparently fitness is good for drug recovery as it releases the same endorphins as crack does.

The more of a routine I got into, the more relaxed I became. Part of that routine would be having one can of tenant's super to get me to sleep at night. One can is enough to fuel a rocket, it's lethal. I only needed the one though to get me off to sleep at night.

Returning from the shop one day, I was sat on the steps outside of the hostel, just chatting to some friends who lived there also. Along came a woman, who I never really got on with. I really didn't need any drama! However, drama was her middle name.

She started to goad me and really wind me up. Back then my fuse was short so before I knew it, we were in fisty cuffs on the middle of the street outside the hostel.

When provoked I would become extremely violent! Not the bitchy, hair pulling and scratching type of violent.

No, I would fight like one of us is dying in the fight and it isn't going to be me! So, it's safe to say I didn't hold back. Finally, staff came and separated us. Returning to my room happily, my ritual of tenants super, book and bed was already past due.

Just as I was settling into bed, there was a loud banging on my door, I jumped up, bricking it. as I reached for my trackys to put on, as I was in my night clothes. The next thing I knew I was being pinned down by at least five police officers, arrested, and brutally bundled into the back of a police van.

What the fudge was going on? Why was I the one being arrested? She started the fight!

Later on, during the interview, the police questioned me about a bite mark on the woman's hand. I laughed at the allegation because in my eyes she was the dog not me.

I didn't bite anyone! She was lying! After the interview I was charged with serious assault. I was lucky that it wasn't attempted murder given my HIV status, I was mortified!

Due to this ridiculous event, I was forced to leave the hostel immediately, so, with no fixed abode I was held in custody till the Monday morning, when the court would decide my fate.

Luckily for me there were staff working on my behalf in the Look Ahead hostel, they managed to get me into Dean Street Hostel. A residence not even fit for humanity.

It was almost immediately after the moment I moved into the hostel at Dean Street that I was ready to score.

What was the point! Every time I tried to break away something just held me back. If this wasn't a sign of the life, I'm destined to live then what was it?

So, jumping back onto the hamster wheel I became reliant on my old friend crack again. And something really strange happened...

One morning just as the sun was coming up, I was smoking in the alley way opposite the Hungerford Project, when JP had announced to all the cats (smokers) that I was HIV, trying to cause trouble.

It was like they scurried away from me like I was going to give it to them, just by touch. There was a black guy that I had never seen before there and he said to me to go with him for a minute, when I walked with him, he said these words...

"It's Okay! You will be healed of HIV just believe "

He prayed over me and then just disappeared down Shaftsbury Avenue towards Piccadilly, never to be seen again. It was a strange encounter, one which I didn't truly understand. How could this man be so bold, to suggest that one day I'm going to be free of HIV!

Ignoring this, I just gave up, admitting defeat I was back on it!

With that live or die mentality, the latter being my number one goal. With no regard to life in general, it had not even entered my mind that I was supposed to appear in court for the serious assault charge that the woman in the hostel, falsely accused me of.

So, it wasn't too long before I found myself being transported in the back of a sweat box, to Holloway prison, on a warrant for failing to surrender. Due to failing to appear meant another charge added to my case. There's no way I was getting out unless I was released on a not guilty.

Straight to detox I went, reuniting with friends from the street, friends that would get them self nicked in the winter to find refuge and retreat from the cold nights.

We used to call it a holiday to Holloway. About two days after my imprisonment to my complete joy, I discovered that the very same woman that got me nicked, had been put into the cell opposite me.

Oh, how I wanted to make her life hell! Everyone on the wing was going to know that this little female dog had got me arrested. Not to mention for false allegations too!

The thing is, within about a week we became friends, then not long after I was moved to the main prison and never saw her again. It had been around a month that I had been inside there was no sign of me getting out either. Then, one morning about five-thirty in the morning.

A screw came and called me for court, to begin with I thought I was dreaming so continued sleeping. Then she returned, to which point I jumped up and got dressed. Slightly confused as I had no court date, I plodded down to the foyer anyway to begin the signing out process.

Strip search at six in the morning, every woman's dream! After a very long day in court, I was released without charge. Somebody in the hostel came forward and testified that she actually bit herself, so, I was released with no further action.

Having been clean for the best part of five weeks, I was completely focused. I wasn't going back to the crack and the drama that followed it.

I moved back into Dean Street hostel and was engaging with support. Unfortunately, this hostel was actually worse than the L.A Victoria when it came to dealers on your doorstep. Temptation got the better of me and I was back on it and worse than ever.

JP and I were now sworn enemies with no going back, he hated me! I slept with his cousin and completely destroyed our relationship. One morning, he caught me off guard as I was clipping a punter, he tried to rob the money off me, and when I stuffed it down my bra, he threw green dye in my face and rode off on his bike. Knowing him, I'm relieved it was dye and not acid!

It was the final straw, I felt violated and unsafe, I couldn't take anymore. No! I was taking a stand this time. I stood in a phone box typed in the Newcastle dialing code, followed with my Aunties telephone number...

After a few rings, she picked up the phone. "Can I come to yours" I asked her, she replied with "of course you can!"

So off I went, back to the place where my life began.

I was twenty-four years old and had the weight of the world on my shoulders, but off I went to Newcastle. Hoping to leave that messed up life once and for all.

Chapter Nine – Finally Free

Back in Newcastle, and fighting strong, I began the full recovery process. I knew no dealers in the area and crack was alien in the northeast, well, decent crack anyway.

Temptation was nowhere to be seen. Whilst I was in prison I was on a small dose of methadone, something like 30ml, I was only prescribed it inside because it's the hardest thing to detox from. The prescription continued when I was released, I just needed to do a transfer of service with the GP service.

However, when I returned to the north east, I chose not to engage with the drug services because I decided to go cold turkey from the methadone. Oh my gosh, it was horrible! Cold sweats, fidgeting continuously, and constant muscle pain.

Not to mention the insomnia, after around six weeks the worst of it was over. I was officially clean! My life was my own again, it was amazing. I loved living at my aunties house.

As always with me, I get settled for a little while, then the cracks begin to appear. Newcastle is my birthplace, the place where most of my traumas from the past took place. All of my demons reside there. So, it wasn't long before I started to get itchy feet.

I missed London! My friends and street family were constantly on my mind. I couldn't settle.

With my insecurities and home sickness getting worse, after around five months in October 2008 life had drawn to a halt and I felt like I was going nowhere, I left Newcastle once again and headed straight to Kings Cross on the train then on to the west end. Although yes, I did go and score as soon as I landed in Soho, I only used for a few days.

I then found myself extremely ill from a severe chest infection in the lobby of Look Ahead Victoria, begging them to take me back in. There is ALWAYS a referral process you have to go through when you are getting into a hostel.

After a short walk to the passage house in Victoria the
referral process was quick,
Kath and Lucy bent over backwards to get me back into
the hostel and succeeded.

I moved in that night. It was around October which is
when I met the next love of my life. He won't appreciate
me mentioning his name, so I'll call him "My Ex!"

My Ex had the gift of the gab, he could charm the birds
out of the trees. That's how he got me, his charm! At
first, I played hard to get, but as the weeks past we
drew closer, until only one thing stood in the way of
moving any further.

That thing being my health status.

I hadn't really had the conversation before, how would
it go?...

Hey, let's sleep together, oh before we do, I have HIV?...

I was terrified to tell him. But after some Dutch courage,
I finally plucked up the nerve to have the conversation

with him. Only to be told he already knew because someone in the hostel already told him.

Then the next thing we knew the deed was done, we had unprotected sex at some point too...

Then a matter of weeks later I found out I was pregnant with his baby. It was just after Christmas when I found out. Happy and ready to be a mum for real this time, I was prepared to do it all on my own. Let's face it the relationship was barely three months old, now there's a pregnancy. When I told My Ex, his emotions were varied, and it took a couple of days for the news to sink in.

A few weeks passed, and it was valentine's day. I was six weeks pregnant, and vomiting blood. Okay, I can't miss this out, I had gone up west on a 24hr binge, all because social services were getting involved to do a risk assessment.

Well, instead of being sensible and behaving myself, I went into complete meltdown mode and went on a binge. Which resulted in me being checked into A&E with blood in my vomit.

The vomiting was scraping the back of my throat which caused my throat to bleed, so, the doctor prescribed me with some sickness medication and told me I could go home after a quick scan.

My Ex had come to the hospital, but I told him to jog on because he was stressing me out. Just after I got rid of My Ex, I was called in for my scan. As I lay there with the cold jelly on my tummy, the sonographer turned to ask me if I knew I was having twins?...

I just burst out crying with joy, TWINS!!

I was the first one in my family to have twins after my nana had hers. I had two for the price of one, I now had a chance to make up for what I lost with Jack. When I told My Ex, he was really angry because he already knew because of me and my big mouth! I had told the whole hostel before I told him.

To be fair he was nowhere to be found, and my excitement got the better of me.

Due to my current predicament, I was moved into the cluster flats, the independent living part of the hostel, where I was to stay until I was seven months gone. I was fortunate to have Kat and Lucy as my keyworkers and Leah as my drug worker, the dream team as I call them.

With their help I stayed focused and kept my eye on the ball. Attending every appointment and assessment the social workers expected me to attend. When I was seven months gone, I had to move on from Look Ahead due to safety reasons.

It was not safe for a heavily pregnant lady to be staying there and the hostel could not risk having me there. So, me and My Ex moved into a temporary B&B just by Marble Arch where we stayed until the 18th of August 2009, which was when we moved into our two bedrooms flat in Churchill Gardens, Pimlico.

Look Ahead Victoria closed later that summer and remains empty to this day! 150+ rooms sat empty and derelict. Just felt I needed to add that.

Two weeks after we moved into the flat, I was booked in for a c-section.

On Tuesday 1ˢᵗ September at 2:59pm Charlie George was born weighing 5lb2oz. Then one minute later his Sister Rebecca Christine joined him weighing 5lb5oz.

As My Ex held Charlie, the nurse handed me Rebecca, I just looked into her eyes, feeling content and complete. I was a mother and this time I was going to get to be a mum too. I had jumped through every hoop during pregnancy, so, there was no reason the twins couldn't come home.

A week after the birth, after some intensive tests and monitoring we were discharged from hospital, time to take my baby's home. A day I longed for, since giving birth to my firstborn Jack. My Ex and I were besotted when we had the twins, we had a fiery relationship from the get-go but when we became parents it brought us closer together.

However, my insecurities would always rear their ugly head and make an appearance, within the stress of being sleep deprived and learning to parent twins, the relationship became impacted in a negative way.

It was early November 2009 I had not long given birth to
the twins. Due to my health status, I was unable to give
birth naturally in case one of the babies contracted the
illness through delivery.

Along with that precaution, there had to be regular
blood tests to monitor my levels of the HIV virus and
also to make sure that the twins were all clear.

Which they were to our relief! When I asked the nurse
about Hepatitis, she informed me they didn't have that
either, or neither did I!

I looked at her in shock and asked her if she was sure, to
which she responded with yes, she was sure and that
the only explanation is, that I have the antibodies in my
blood, the antibodies must have fought and cured the
virus.

Okay, so I had to get this straight I didn't have Hepatitis
just HIV. No plausible explanation I was just cured. "Hep
B can be cured by antibodies, but Hep C, can't! Only
medication can cure the latter. Not really grasping the
fact that I had been cured of an illness that is only

curable by taking a drug for twelve months called interferon, yet I'm cured without it.

So, this was it, perfection! Neither of the twins had contracted any virus and I was cured too! This had to be a miracle, right?...

Due to my instability as a young adult, I was watched like a hawk by social services but after bending over backwards and proving my ability to parent, Social services discharged the case after six months.

A day of complete victory for me and Leah my drug worker. She came with me to court. It was one of the best days of my life. The judge said I deserved a pat on the back, for the complete reversal of ways since my battle with the local authority over Jack.

Proud was an understatement. The first two years of mine and my ex's relationship were fine, we argued but we always made up quickly. Then one day in February 2012 My Ex decided he didn't want me anymore and cheated on me, he just disappeared for days on end to go and be with a different woman.

I found out quite quickly, I'm not stupid I knew he had cheated, where else would he have been! I left him the day I found out, taking the kids to my aunties house in Newcastle.

I feel like I need to clarify, my current relationship with the twin's dad is rarely a good one, and we remain amicable now for the sake of the twins, I have tried to avoid going into too much detail of my time with this man. For my own reasons. I would rather just skim past the three years I was with him.

In Newcastle I was fast tracked through the housing and on the waiting list for a house.

While I was there, I hit rock bottom, completely broken from the recent events. I turned to a different drug, this time I started hammering the speed. Along with the speed I was drinking loads, I just didn't care. Not long after social services were once again involved.

My chaotic behavior was resulting in me getting myself noticed by the authorities! I had to get my act together. Days before the twins third birthday, I decided to return to my flat in Pimlico, thinking it would shake social services, instead it made me look even more unstable.

The thing is not only had I moved my children back to the center of an abusive relationship, but I had also informed the police and the authorities that My Ex was an abusive partner whilst I was still in a place of anger.

Which made things extremely difficult when I tried to allow him to see the children. Social services provided me with a no contact order. My Ex was not allowed near the children.

When I returned, I was fooled by an illusion that My Ex and I could rekindle our love and be a happy family again, My Ex on the other hand thought he could play me and his mistress at the same time.

I knew he was with her, yet he was living in my house, sleeping in my bed, I began to find solace at the bottom of the bottle, letting thoughts of them together mess with my head.

The past twelve months had been hard, my twin's dad had cheated on me and it was time for a clean break. I had two choices I could either move to Tooting where my best friend Tasha lived, or I could move to Wallasey for a complete fresh start.

The decision was a tough one because I would have loved to have been closer to Tasha, but the logical decision was to move to Wallasey. Once the decision was made the house hunting began.

I wasn't sure how I was going to pay for the move, being on benefits I knew where to look for help. I applied for a community care grant and budgeting loan through the social fund department of the social security office.

Once the forms are received, you can get a decision within six weeks. I applied for both expecting a knock back on at least one.

Whilst I waited for my answer by post, I searched online for possible houses to rent, although I was quickly becoming deflated at needing a deposit and a month's rent upfront, I wasn't giving up! So, I then decided to have a look on the Westminster.gov website to see what help I could get. To my surprise, I stumbled across a section that mentioned a private landlord scheme, that went on to say that if you relinquish your tenancy with the Westminster council and go private in another area, the council will pay you to hand in your keys.

The price they pay varies, depending on whether or not you are in temporary or permanent housing if you live in a permanent house or flat you get £10,000 but if you live in a temporary accommodation you can get £3000 provided you didn't have any rent arrears.

"Kerching!" I was only in a temporary flat so was only given three grand, but it was more than enough to get me started in Wallasey.

I found a three-bedroom house pretty quickly and Sandy viewed it for me and accepted immediately. I was ready to go I just needed to borrow the money until mine came through, to put up front for the new house and I was set.

A day or two after the tenancy was agreed I received two brown envelopes in the post, I knew what they were before I opened them, I opened them in a hurry to see what they said.

To my complete surprise I had been awarded £600 budgeting loan and a £900 community care grant.

Winner, winner chicken dinner! That was a total of four and a half grand to move up to Wallasey, all handed to me without stress, there had to be a mix up in the universe somewhere, these sorts of good things don't usually happen to people like me.

So off we went for a complete fresh start, just me and the twins "The three musketeers."

Chapter Ten – A New Life

The day of the move ran smoothly, although we got caught on the train with a load of football fans trying to get to the match.

We arrived safely at our new home around 2pm. I remember feeling like it was the most content feeling I had felt since giving birth. A brand-new start for me and my little cherubs!

Not only had we stepped into a brand-new life, but we had stepped into a proper family too.

The children's great auntie was very eager to take the twins to Sunday school every week, I was quite happy to have a break so I would stay at home and chill while they were gone.

I would insist that I do believe in God, but I don't do church. What was the point of going to some middle-class service, to be looked upon as some dirty little ex junkie?

No way was I opening myself up to that judgement. If only I knew then what I know now.

My life seemed so perfect, everything just felt like it was meant to be. I now had a supportive family that were encouraging me to make better choices. I had a determination to be the best mum I could be to my children, there was nothing that could lead me back to that darkness now.

Trouble is, the loneliness started to creep in, because I knew no-one and I began to feel home sick, which made me resent my new family in Wallasey for suggesting the idea of me moving there. They had done absolutely nothing wrong I just became extremely insecure.

Whenever I start getting close to anyone, I instantly feel like I must sever all ties before I get hurt. So, I began to lash out for no reason causing negativity within the family unit. Upsetting everyone around me.

Then one day everything changed, I was invited on a day out with the children's church, a non-religious fun day in a park in Warrington.

I accepted because it did sound fun and the twins would enjoy it. There were two double decker busses filled with people that were all attending this church day out.

As I chatted to the lady in front of me on the bus, I realized that actually, these Christian folk are not really that judgmental after all. In fact, they seem very accepting and inviting.

I can't deny this really put me at ease about the whole churchy thing.

A few weeks passed from the big church day out and the children were continuously attending every Sunday, as I chilled at home enjoying the break.

It was then September...

Every year the church has a gift giving service for all of the children and young people that attend the Sunday school. Well, the twins were too going to receive a gift.

They were only four at the time, but I would never miss anything like that, it was like a little school assembly where they were called to the front for a little gift from the church, which is usually a bible or story book.

So, there I was sitting in the back row of this little family church in Wallasey, completely out of my depth when, Charlie walks up to me and asks if I can come to church every week...

Erm.... What do you say to your four-year-old when he asks that kind of question?...

"We'll See."

Apparently, it was not up to me though!

Every week from that day on, I felt a deep urge within me to get ready on Sunday morning and attend church with the children.

I actually enjoyed it!! The songs and the stories from the Bible had me fixated every week; I was so hungry for more. As the months past the more I felt myself changing as a person. Like the old me was slipping away and a new me was surfacing. From that first time in

September, through to the following April, I grew
deeper into the whole church thing.

On the last Sunday of April just days before my 30TH
birthday I declared my love for Jesus and was baptized
in water. A feeling so immense, one that I could never
forget. I was a new creation, washed clean in the water.
The old had left me as the new became rooted.

The coming months were turbulent to say the least. I was doing everything within me to stay on this new path of faith.

I obtained a voluntary position at a Christian youth work service, with the drug and alcohol awareness team. I was part of the worship band at church and attending every service and small group I could cram in.

I loved this brand-new life. Nothing could ever take this joy from me. I was happy and content with all that I had. Over time though cracks appeared, as they always do when I get settled for any long period of time. I had become very close to a group of the ladies from the church, a little too close maybe.

In September 2015, precisely two years into my conversion, I had fallen out with the group of ladies. It was a bad argument that even now the relationships have never fully recovered.

There was a big church weekend away to MCYC in Wales. It was something the church does every other year to build on the fellowship of the church. This year someone had very kindly paid for the children and I to attend the weekend away. It had been done anonymously as a blessing.

Even to this day, I'm totally blown away by the generosity of that person! That weekend changed my life forever...The weekend was catered to bring us together as a church. There was a guest speaker who would bring us a message over the course of the weekend.

I remember feeling awkward anyway because I was surrounded by the ladies who I had recently fell out with. Then the Pastor guy starts his sermon for the weekend, based on the book of Romans.

By the time, the weekend was over I was in pieces, completely distraught by all of my wrong doings in the past. All of my sins and failures washing over me, making me feel completely unworthy of God's love.

I ran to my chalet toilet and locked the door, where I began to sob uncontrollably. How can God love me, after all I have done?

How can He forgive me when I hold so much of a grudge for the ladies across the green, outside the chalets? I heard a knock on the bathroom door, it was Liz. She was asking if I was okay... No, I said as I sobbed through the door. I was on my knees heartbroken and I had no idea why.

Liz and I spoke for the whole journey home, it took around two hours. I can't quite remember what we spoke about, but it brought me peace and clarity.

Later that night, I felt compelled to put my favorite worship song on, so I did...

WOW!! I must have looked like a raving lunatic, dancing round my living room singing "Praise the Lord" "Thank You Jesus" It was as if I was possessed or something...

After this brief encounter, I felt the need to share my experience, so, I messaged my friend Claire. Completely away with the fairy's I typed out what had just happened, starting with "Claire I think I have just been saved" I remember I was shaking whilst I waited on her reply.

"You already are saved" The reply came through... "You have just been spiritually saved."

Huh?

So, it may seem that I had encountered the Holy Spirit in a spiritual baptism, something I had no clue about. My life transformed from this moment on, a 360-degree turn, that could have only ever have been made possible, by the hand of God.

As I look back in my life, I can't count the amount of times that God has showed up, trying to bring me back on to a path of righteousness. Now I had witnessed a supernatural encounter in a spiritual baptism. Oh my gosh the world is going to think I'm bonkers!

Chapter Eleven – No Turning Back

After that night, I felt different, it felt like the old me had gone, like I was a new creation or something. I heard about a little coffee shop in Wallasey Village called Community Soul, it was a Christian not for profit community coffee shop. I loved it from the get-go! When I had discovered they were looking for volunteers I jumped straight on it and contacted the manager Sam.

While I worked there, I felt myself becoming more grounded and in control. Along with that placement I was also helping out at the local homeless charity, community spirit. Which was a drop in and food bank for those in need, moonlighting as a soup run for the homeless.

I finally felt like I was turning it all around, with no turning back.

I was settled and growing from strength to strength! I had joined a new church and stepped fully into my mission to share the word of Jesus with everyone. The thing is not everyone wants to know! I have been ridiculed and tested, many times but I stood strong in my faith.

In February 2017 I started my first ever paid job as a youth worker and outreach manager, for the church of England. I loved my job; community is of strong importance to me.

Then, in 2018 I decided to start blogging about my lived experiences, in hope to shed a light on the issues surrounding homelessness. At first, I was half-heartedly writing as a healing process, thinking helping others will help me. Yeah, that kind of works, but not fully.

In October 2018 I was visiting my best friend Tasha in London and I thought why not meet up with some friends while I'm down there and make some connections. I was now stepping out fully in my mission to eradicate homelessness by becoming a voice of hope.

I met with Kath, my old keyworker from L.A Victoria, she was the head of outreach at St, Mungo's now and I wanted to pick her brains about some stuff along with having a good old catch up. Whilst meeting with Kath, she told me that her boss Petra was dying to meet me and wanted to know if I would like to speak at an event at the heart of London business alliance.

I was thrilled at the invitation and jumped for the opportunity. I met with Petra the next day and a few days later I was standing on Piccadilly on my old pitch ready to go into the Royal Academy of Arts to give a talk on my experience on rough sleeping, in Piccadilly.

The fact that this talk was in the exact same location on google maps, to where I slept alone on the street's years before, was no coincidence. It was a moment of raw emotion along with extreme self-empowerment. I was standing in a moment of revelation, my life had spun 360 degrees, and at that moment it all became real.
I walked into the reception area and up the stairs, feeling like the odd one out, among all of the business-like people in the room, I made way for the coffee cart, then hid in the corner, waiting for Petra.

As soon as I saw Petra's face, I became a nervous wreck, the emotion swept over me like a tornado. I got myself together with some encouraging words from Petra and the next thing I knew, it was time to go into the talk.

I sat at the front to make it easier for when I had to get up and talk. The meeting was packed out, I was a complete nervous wreck. There was a panel on the little stage where Petra sat behind me to the right.

It was my first time speaking at an event that was so grand and influential. I nervously said my bit, then sat down. After I spoke, I sat down feeling awesome, feeling like I had just fulfilled a purpose. That day I travelled back to Liverpool on a complete high. I felt like tables were turning and doors were opening in a place not yet seen. I was feeling all fired up and ready to really step out.

A couple of weeks past then I received a call from Petra, St, Mungo's had been chosen by the Times Newspaper to be a participant in their annual Christmas appeal. They wanted to interview various people that had experienced homelessness and she wanted to know if I would like to do it.

Shut the front door!!

Erm, yes! I would love to have my story published in the Times! Buzzing was an understatement. Sandy had the kid's, and my travel and hotel was paid for. I felt like a queen!

I met with the journalist from the Times in the Waterstones on Piccadilly, there was a lovely lady called Hannah with me, she worked for the comms department at Mungo's. Again, it was strange, because I used to sleep in the doorway outside and take drugs in the toilet of the actual building, I was sitting in. Seriously, how times have changed.

After the interview we were joined by the photographer who took some shots of me in the various pitches I slept in and where I used to beg. I can't really explain it, but it was strange, it was like I was talking about a different person completely, that life is on the opposite end of the spectrum compared to what it was that particular day and even more so now. Once we finished up, I went for a coffee with Hannah, before heading off to the tube on my route home to Liverpool.

Chapter Twelve – Born Ready

Ever since I was a young girl, I have always had a fascination with words. I love how you can play with different words to make the most beautiful sonnets and songs. The old me loved the power of words in a battle and was so eager to use them as my weapon to win. The new me loves the power and encouragement words can bring from sharing a story...

Part of me feels that I was born to write this story, to spread hope among the nations. To bring freedom and deliverance to those that are trapped in similar circumstances. So, in February 2019 I decided to self-publish my first book under the title of Blessed Assurance as an eBook on Amazon.

Impulsive being my middle name, that book was nowhere near ready! The cover was hideous, and the content was lacking! After a couple of months and a few requests for a paperback, I decided to revise the book adding extra chapters, renaming it and redesigned the cover.

In August 2019, my paperback Gutter to Glory was ready and sold a hundred copies in the first month. The reviews were overwhelmingly encouraging, and I knew that I had finally found what I was born to do. Despite selling like hotcakes the first month, it's a hard graft getting the word out alone.

Without any support from a publisher and just me doing the promoting I became slightly disheartened as I could not see any progress going forward. After six months I was ready to admit defeat on my writing career, I had few followers engaging in my blog and the sales were 1 a month if that.

I started to feel like nobody was interested in what I had to say, maybe I'm not loud enough...

Then came my days in Parliament.

*****

The first visit to Parliament was so last minute I barely had time to pack, let alone prepare.

Tasha had so kindly agreed to letting me stay at her house in Mitcham, so I was quite close to Westminster. I made sure I left in plenty of time, because I have never been to that specific part of Parliament before so wanted to make sure I wasn't late. Instead, I was forty-five minutes early!

I got a little lost at first, surprisingly! I know my way around Westminster like the back of my hand, from being a resident on the pavements there throughout my teenage and early adult years. When I finally arrived at my destination, my stomach dropped as the realization hit me.

Oh my gosh, I'm speaking in Parliament, "pinch, pinch, ouch!" I was already feeling petrified, then I noticed the revolving door with security on the other side, it was actually more full-on than the airport with the security measures. My stomach dropped again, I hate revolving doors, I get scared in case I get stuck. I wasn't really fazed by the metal detectors though.

Now the thing is, without meaning to sound out of turn. Not all people in Parliament want to help for the right reasons. So, I did get an incy bit frustrated shall we say by some of the questions in the room. I'm very defensive too when it comes to rough sleeping! To me, every single person sleeping on the streets is a human being, with a right to love and respect.

When approaching the issue of homeless, it should always come from a place of compassion and not obligation. At the end of the meeting Petra and I went for lunch in the Terrace Cafeteria with Winnie who helped to organize the event.

It was mental, we were pretty much underneath Big Ben, it was quite a mind-blowing experience walking through the same corridor's as some of the most famous politicians and prime ministers.

Now would be a good time to say, until the moment I stepped into Portcullis House at Parliament, politics was number one on my list for hates. For years I resented the government. In my eyes they failed me when I was in care, then they stole my child, this was my opportunity to have my say!

I was there to plant some seeds, in hope to see some system change. Not get involved in political affairs. After leaving Petra, I set off home to Liverpool, until the next time I was invited to speak on the 3rd ^{of} March 2020.

There were more people at the second event than the first and I was a lot more prepared for the meeting. However, that was the beginning of the pandemic so there were some very important people missing from the meeting. I left feeling accomplished though and received a very moving review from Jacob Reece Mogg, so I came away happy.

The day after my second parliamentary visit, lockdown began! Without sounding ignorant, life has dried up for everyone. The world we once knew is a distant memory and a new life of sterilization and social distancing is a new norm for everyone.

Chapter Thirteen – The Perfect Ending

Lockdown one, hit me hard, having PTSD I struggled to stay busy after my bold encounter in Parliament, so all of the triggers that I usually occupy with busyness were wide open and ready to attack.

I also have an emotional personality disorder, ADHD, along with anxiety and depression, so it is safe to say that the forced isolation took its toll on me. For the best part, I stayed in bed feeling sorry for myself. Depressed, angry, lonely, and sad.

The twins spent a lot of time at their nans house, when I was struggling to even look after myself. I felt so useless and incapable to see how far I had come. My mental health had spiraled backwards into a place of insecurity and mental isolation.

I finally started to come out of my slump in August as things were starting to return to normal. I was on a new medication, that seemed to be working and I started to be my happy bubbly self again. As we all know, it wasn't long before Lockdown 2.0 was on the horizon.

As soon as I had heard on the news that we were going into a circuit breaker lockdown, the joy drained instantly from my body. Not again! The last one was hard enough, I'm not sure I could do another.

Early November 2020, days before the lockdown, I received a message on Facebook from a lady I had no connections to. Because we weren't friends, the message went straight to the message requests folder.

A few days later, the same lady popped up on my Facebook business page. I opened the second message, and nothing could ever prepare me for its contents…

Basically, it said hi I'm Jacks adopted mum and she thought I would like to know, that my son would like to connect with me! What the fudge!!!!!!!!!!

I replied with a couple of messages like oh my gosh, I have waited sixteen years for this.

Another one of those "PINCH PINCH OUCHHH" moments. No way, this was real! Two years before I can legally reach out, here I am standing in my hallway shaking uncontrollably as I send my son a friend request on Facebook, which he instantly accepts.

I rang Sandy and started sobbing down the phone "Sandy, Jacks been in touch" she told me to calm down and get round to hers, she only lives a street away. When I arrived, she offered me a coffee and I asked for something stronger, so she poured me a vodka and orange.

I still feel shocked and overwhelmed, and in honesty it is hard to explain the feeling of being complete. Eleven years before, I chose to fight for this actual day. I got clean and out of the life of homelessness, so that one day my boy would find me and have a reason to want to know me.

Its been difficult because we live 200 miles apart, and we haven't had the chance to meet in person, I have been very grateful for the ability to video call though. I now just long for the day, I finally get to hug my son.

How's that for a happy ever after?!

You have reached the present day in my story, it's January 2021 we are all stuck in lockdown 3.0 a life most of us are now used to. Although I'm still not living my happy ever after with some handsome prince on my arm, I lack nothing.

I'm a strong, wise, and independent woman, doing what I can to finally bring system change and I'm doing my bit for world peace. I am very excited to be speaking in another parliamentary meeting this month and looking forward to whatever comes next.

As I close this book, I want to leave on this, my life is living proof that anything is possible. We ALL have an inner strength to overcome if we have the right encouragement and nurture and not to mention faith...

The Last Word

In looking back through my life there are many gaps to my story, things that I may have chosen to forget about. Traumas I may have even forced myself to forget about.

The reason I wrote this book, was to highlight on why someone might end up homeless on the streets and why they choose to stay homeless. Not to mention provoke thought for system change.

I thought a good way to really end this book would be with a little Q&A session to clear up any questions you may have. Please note, what you are about to read is solely my opinion from which I have concluded from my own lived experiences. Please feel free to conclude your own opinion of what the answers should be.

*****

Question One – What could young-peoples-services have done differently to prevent the absconding and youth homelessness?

When all children hit a certain age, they become hormonal and difficult to manage, adding the fact of being a child in care it becomes a target for so many emotional insecurities. Add again the undiagnosed ADHD, then you have a dangerous combination that requires a completely different type of nurture.

Due to the lack of understanding towards mental health in young people, led to a failure in me receiving the correct nurture in my care plan. Instead of being supported, I was written off as a problem child with behavioral issues.

Therefore, I conclude that it should be mandatory that children's social services undergo full mental health training as part of their role. I also think that foster carers and adoption services too should make this a compulsory learning. In doing so, this will equip them in handling individual cases sufficiently and correctly.

By understanding the mental health of young people, the right support can be accessed, and preventions can be put into place to stop the issues from escalating.

Question Two – Why was I so disengaged.

I could honestly write a ten-page essay on this question! I'll try and keep it short and effective. Ever since I was a young child I have had to engage with different services. Mental health workers, social workers, therapists, psychiatrists, the list continues.

Each service will refer you to one and other, but in the process share very little information with each other. So, when you start a new service or get a new keyworker you have to go over and over everything! Personally, I wanted to forget and block it all out, like many people I knew back then. The repetitive cycles through engagement were too hard to bare. It was easier to disengage.

Every so often I would have to start a new service, or I would get a new key worker, there was never any consistency in the support being offered, which led to me becoming inconsistent in my engagement.

Communication was difficult too, having ADHD my communication is lacking anyway. Having to be repetitive with different people and services constantly my whole life, made it extremely difficult for me to maintain engagement. I lost interest and found it extremely draining going over my life, time and time again.

Question Three – What made me start engaging?

It took a long time to get to a point of asking for help. The important thing to consider is that you can't help anyone who doesn't want to help themself. It wasn't until I had hit rock bottom that I asked for help.

The right services were always available when I finally chose to access them fully. I was lucky that my keyworkers approached me with love and compassion something that was rare within services. The very qualities I had craved my whole life. I didn't need a service or a roof over my head! I needed someone to show me I deserved to be loved.

Knowing that there were services available for me to access in my timing was always a glimmer of hope. It was always heartwarming to come across a homeless service worker that was patiently waiting to assist my needs from a place of compassion and not a wage slip.

I believe it was the homely feel to hostels that made me engage. Wherever I felt warmth I felt drawn. The Look Ahead Hostels were both very inviting and homely. I was encouraged to make better choices. Then through the Hungerford Drug Project I was provided with new addictions like smoothy club or women's group during the drop-in services, when they came to the hostel.

Question Four – What can you do to help someone who is homeless?

A lot of people ask me this question and my spontaneous non-thought-out response is always "Love Them". Many rough sleepers have forgotten what it even feels like to be loved. My favorite saying at the moment is "Love thy neighbor as thy self" well, what if you don't actually love yourself?

Basically, you become a shell of emptiness. Where sleeping on the streets becomes a feeling of being better off than even living at all. The longer someone has been on the street, the harder it will be to reach them.

With all hope lost for them, the best way to help them is by reminding them they are worthy of love and by reminding them that they are better than their circumstance. It really is easier said than done! But just think of how children resist and push buttons to see how far they can get?

When you are trying to help someone get off the streets, they are just like children! Numb to emotion, because every single person they ever trusted has hurt them or let them down. So, they will push every single button to see how far they can push before you abandon them.

My advice is love them unconditionally and don't back down. If they see you standing ground, you will see them open up.

The next thing I will add is if you buy a hot chocolate and then go and sit and talk with a homeless person whilst they drink it, that will most likely mean more to them than money itself. Although, I strongly advise against it, if you do want to give money, please do so on the understanding that it is likely to be going on a substance that will help them forget their past and ease their pain.

Question Five – What can outreach services do to increase engagement?

To be honest, this question has multiple answers from me. I had to add this one because it is highly important, in terms of system change. The relationship between service provider and service user is a tricky one and its probably the biggest barrier that stands in the way of a successful engagement.

My first tip would be, don't come weighing in like an authoritative figure or just another professional. That is an instant red flag. Taking the trust issues into account, and the uncontrollable urges to forget the past.

By coming in as another professional, you are delivering a wrong message. If you want someone to engage with you, there needs to be a reason other than "just doing your job" for them to want to engage with you. Many rough sleepers in particular choose to not engage with services for the same reason as me, a fear of being let down again.

Treat them as a friend or like how you would treat your neighbor or local shop keeper, and not like just another client.

Think of it like this, your in a pub or restaurant and some random person comes up to your table. You are just minding your own business, trying to get on with your life in your own little bubble! Then this stranger starts reminding you of everything your trying to run away from and forget, in an attempt to make you face it...

How would you feel? Honestly?

Personally, I would be thinking jog-on mate you don't know me...

Well, that's exactly what it is like. When I used to be pitched up, either begging, reading, or bedding down for the night. That was me getting on with my life and trying to forget.

Every time I engaged in conversation with the street workers, I would go round in circles, it was easier to tell them to f-off. I get now, that they were only trying to do their job, but I didn't want another professional trying to interfere.

Also, let me add! If it is a regular that you know struggles to engage, just stop, and chat without even mentioning them getting in somewhere or accessing services. That will show them you are talking to them as a person and not just another statistic or bed to fill. Chances are they will then come and ask you for help.

I know that there are safeguarding rules put into place for a reason and I completely agree that safety for both parties must be considered at all times! But you can safely change your approach and delivery and come in from an angle of compassion rather than obligation. Can't you?

My next tip would be, create a space for people to come on their own terms...

Back in my days on the street, there were drop-ins everywhere, where you could go eat and socialize in a safe space, on your own terms with no pressure. Services that had staff and keyworkers to support in every area of need. By the mid 2000's most of those services had closed due to funding cuts. The closure of those services meant a rise in disengagement.

The key ingredient in any successful rehabilitation is positive nurture. If a long-term rough sleeper, finally gets off of the streets they need to be nurtured like a child. Helping change old patterns by replacing them with new edifying ones can be really beneficial.

Drop-ins provided workshops and social activities that catered for those nurturing needs and enhanced self-esteem.

I believe by reinventing those drop-in services you are allowing a space for growth in trust and also you are allowing a space for personal growth too. You are also creating a platform to identify any other areas of need; therefore, you have an opening to subtly offer support.

Question Six – What could homeless services have done differently to enhance engagement?

When I was on the street, there were a lot of homeless people. Now, the numbers have multiplied greatly. Obviously, something is not working right?

When you go to the doctors or the hospital, what is the worst part of the visit for you? For me it's the wait. When I was homeless that was the thing that took up most of our time, the waiting.

We would have to wait hours on end just to see the GP at Great Chapel Street, because it was the only one in the area that was equipped for homelessness related issues. Then we would have to wait on the doorstep at The Connections from 8:30am to guarantee a slot to get in for a shower, food and the use of the washer and dryer.

You also had to get your name down quick for a bed space too, if any had become available that morning. So, it was crucial that you were at the front of the que when the doors at St' Martins opened.

In the early 2000's The Connection at St Martins which was the youth homeless service that catered for 16–25-

year-olds, merged with the adult service next door at St Martins in the Fields next to the crypt.

I believe that although the intentions may have seemed right in merging, personally I believe it was probably the worst thing that happened. Gaps were created and disengagement became easier.

Before the merge, the staff at connections were able to take a time out and come chat with you, play pool and take interest in you as an individual. There was a healthy balance between staff and young people. The service was easy to engage with because of the family and close nit community element to it.

Then after the merge it became unbearable to engage because the number of homeless people accessing the service had multiplied greatly. The healthy balance had become chaos and the staff that we young people once knew became strangers in the busyness.

My point here is, there must always be a healthy balance between outreach workers and clients within the service. If there is a rise in numbers accessing the service, its clear that a duplicate service must be created. Trying to cram everyone in to one service, messes with the dynamic, which creates invisible barriers in terms of rehabilitation support.

Then taking a look at Look Ahead Victoria, the services available were on top form! However, there were over two-hundred people on one site and only a couple of handfuls of those were staff.

It was chaos! Daily, you would see more drama than on a Jeremey Kyle show, with staff running up and down castle lane with walkie talkies trying to calm substance fueled altercations. The thing is they were not equipped, nor were they in a place of authority which led to police regularly being called.

At least a hundred of the residents were addicts and they bounced off each other. It is like putting a classroom of children together, all with varying complex needs. It can be uncontrollable right?

What do you do? Find a way to tailor individual support and decrease the case load by duplicating the service this will definitely make room for engagement. Most importantly all staff must be trained at the level of complexity required to handle the case load.

The battle of rehabilitation is a tough fight for both service provider and service user; therefore, a level of empathetic understanding is essential. All homeless outreach services need to be equipped with the right knowledge of the psychology behind the actions of a rough sleeper.

Understanding that resolving homelessness is not just about filling beds and clearing streets! It is about reconditioning a persons thinking, leading them to make better choices...

That's the end of the Q&A!

So, I'll wrap it up on this. I was very anti-service when I was lost on the street, you have read my reasons why. In reflection I see there were services available throughout my journey, but there was always a common obstacle in the way "Lack of Trust". Plus, I didn't want to help myself! I had no reason to change, nobody loved me, and I hated myself!

Then one day I was shown love and encouragement not to mention consistency and it all changed! Love really does make the world go round, and by loving those who don't know how to love themselves, you are spreading little seeds of hope.

We all know what happens to a seed if you give it the right kind of nurture don't, we?...

To be continued..

Printed in Great Britain
by Amazon

29154958R00106